P9-CBV-379

DATE DUE

			PRINTED IN U.S.A.

Solon Public Library
320 W. Main
Solon, IA 52333

At Issue

When Is Free Speech Hate Speech?

Other Books in the At Issue Series

At Issue

When Is Free Speech Hate Speech?

Martin Gitlin, Book Editor

GREENHAVEN PUBLISHING

Published in 2018 by Greenhaven Publishing, LLC
353 3rd Avenue, Suite 255, New York, NY 10010

Copyright © 2018 by Greenhaven Publishing, LLC

First Edition

All rights reserved. No part of this book may be reproduced in any form
without permission in writing from the publisher, except by a reviewer.

Articles in Greenhaven Publishing anthologies are often edited for length to meet page
requirements. In addition, original titles of these works are changed to clearly present
the main thesis and to explicitly indicate the author's opinion. Every effort is made to
ensure that Greenhaven Publishing accurately reflects the original intent of the authors.
Every effort has been made to trace the owners of the copyrighted material.

Cover image: Ivan Kotliar/Shutterstock.com

Library of Congress Cataloging-in-Publication Data

Names: Gitlin, Marty, editor.
Title: When is free speech hate speech? / Martin Gitlin, book editor.
Description: New York : Greenhaven Publishing, 2018. | Series: At issue |
  Includes bibliographical references and index. | Audience: Grades 9-12.
Identifiers: LCCN 2017009086| ISBN 9781534500785 (pbk.) | ISBN
  9781534500778 (library bound)
Subjects: LCSH: Hate speech--Law and legislation--United States--Juvenile
  literature. | Freedom of speech--United States--Juvenile literature. |
  Hate speech--Law and legislation--Juvenile literature.
Classification: LCC KF9345 .W44 2017 | DDC 323.44/30973--dc23
LC record available at https://lccn.loc.gov/2017009086

Manufactured in the United States of America

Website: http://greenhavenpublishing.com

Contents

Introduction

The First Amendment to the United States Constitution was intended to provide clarity in regard to freedom of speech. The ink-to-paper tenets set forth in 1789 established an unalienable right for all Americans. And it has been embraced ever since as a beacon and one of the guiding principles on which the country was founded.

But thirteen years before the Constitution was written, the Declaration of Independence featured a phrase that had destroyed the possibility of absolutism. It has been proven that unhindered freedom of speech can spur events that prevent others from attaining "life, liberty and the pursuit of happiness." When freedom of speech is interpreted as freedom to express hate, it is the duty of lawmakers and courts to decide if it infringes upon the ability of an individual or group to indeed live up to the ideals as stated in 1776. The blurring between free speech and hate speech has been debated for more than a century.

Hate speech is defined as words that offend, threaten, or insult based on race, religion, national origin, sexual orientation, disability or other traits that most Americans accept make their country wonderfully diverse. The huge majority of public speeches given even by the most polarizing liberal or conservative in American society are rarely construed as espousing hate. Such utterances are generally reserved by right-wing or religious extremists, many of whom believe in white supremacy or embrace a perverted view of God as hating groups such as Muslims or gays. But where does hate speech end and "fighting words" begin? And should extremists be allowed to express their views openly in the first place?

The gray area has never been transformed to black or white. Libertarians that claim free speech includes hate speech believe that placing restrictions on one person weakens the rights of all. They might recognize that "fighting words" – a phrase used by the

Supreme Court in 1942 to establish a limitation to free speech – promotes violence to such a degree that it is a sufficient reason to rein in that right. But they also feel strongly that hate speech should not be restricted by the government unless it directly causes a threat to peace.

An opposite view is embraced by communitarians. They believe that free speech takes a back seat to the security of a community and all its citizens. They reacted with dismay, for instance, when the American Civil Liberties Union (ACLU) fought for the right of neo-Nazis to march in a predominantly Jewish neighborhood of Skokie, Illinois, in 1977. Their view is that hate speech should not be allowed when it is being spewed by those who seek to prevent individuals or groups from being treated with dignity and respect. Libertarians claim that such restrictions would severely limit free speech and be subject to interpretations of intent that would be impossible to be agreed upon.

The controversy intensified after Donald Trump began his presidential campaign in 2016. His rhetoric and stated views about closing the doors to Muslim refugees, sending illegal immigrants back to Mexico and building a wall to prevent others from entering the country motivated extremists such as white nationalists to rally by his side. It can be argued that Trump had no intention to legitimize those who hate, but the result was an awakening of the free speech/hate speech debate through their words.

History provides arguments on both sides. The wide-open Weimar Republic in Germany of the 1920s and early 1930s promoted unlimited free speech. The result, particularly after World War I and during the depression, was the rise of extremist views that were openly expressed. The most effective speaker during that era was Nazi Party leader Adolf Hitler, who made no secret of his hatred of Jews and Communists, whom he linked together. His hate speeches drove supporters to violently attack perceived enemies of Germany. Hitler, however, banned free speech after taking power in 1933. One could argue that hate speeches that could be perceived as threatening against Hitler and his Fascist followers would have saved the world from the Holocaust and a war that killed at least fifty million people.

Should the German government have allowed Hitler to speak in public? Should its leaders have trusted that there were not enough adherents to his hatred of Jews and others to pose a threat to society? That is the crux of the debate in modern-day America. It is a particularly contentious dispute on college campuses throughout the country, where many students have argued that speakers espousing hate should not be invited and others have embraced the right of guests to express unpopular viewpoints.

One such case indicates that a compromise between both positions is possible if the huge majority that are sickened by hateful extremism make their voices heard. The incident revolved around white supremacist Matt Hale, who was scheduled to speak at the University of Illinois in Springfield in 2001. The school neither banned him nor discouraged students from attending. Hale proved unable to deliver his message as effectively as he would have liked through the cackles and catcalls of students that interrupted him constantly. One interracial couple embraced and kissed in front of him, in the opinion of many at the event expressing without words a message more powerful than anything Hale uttered during his two-hour appearance. Though some argued that the hecklers prevented Hale from exercising his right to free speech, others claimed that the same right to free speech was exercised by the students.

A similar scenario played out fifteen years later at Texas A&M University, where white nationalist Richard Spencer spoke and later claimed he had through his words provoked the students to see the world differently. What he had triggered, however, was unification against racism. Thousands of students showed up at a competing event at the school's football stadium to voice their opposition to Spencer.

Such rare triumphs for both libertarians and communitarians do not solve the problem. At issue are the questions swirling around the gray area. How is hate speech defined? When does the expression of hate move into the realm of "fighting words" that become a threat to individuals and groups? Should the government or Supreme Court take a stronger stand in the debate and emerge with more concrete laws that provide a strict definition? What would be the harm to society and freedoms if hateful rhetoric was simply banned? Could such laws be effectively enforced?

The viewpoints in *At Issue: When Is Free Speech Hate Speech?* present arguments from all sides of the issue. Only through thorough knowledge of the subject and the grasping of opposing viewpoints can one form a learned and legitimate opinion. The purpose of his resource is to raise the level of consciousness and understanding about the free speech/hate speech debate to that it can be discussed intelligently in the hope of finding a solution that will help America live up to its ideals.

1

Where Does Free Speech End and Hate Speech Begin?

Joyce Arthur

Joyce Arthur is founder and executive director of the Abortion Rights Coalition of Canada, a national political pro-choice group. She is also a writer and self-avowed feminist, atheist and abortion rights activist.

The author of this article espouses the belief that the spectrum of hate speech, as it relates to the law, should be expanded. She claims that its illegality must extend beyond the incitement of violence to the expression of ridicule against various groups of people based on such characteristics as race, religion, gender, and sexual orientation. She further asserts that broadening the classification of hate speech would lead to a more tolerant society.

The popular catchphrase of free speech defenders is a quote attributed to Voltaire: "I disapprove of what you say, but I will defend to the death your right to say it." Civil libertarians often defend and support the notion that the right to freely express offensive opinions is a bedrock human right that should not be abridged except under very narrow circumstances—typically for hate speech that directly incites violence against a person or group of persons. However, I support broader prosecution of hate speech—defined here as speech that disparages a person or class of persons based on an immutable characteristic (colour, race,

"The Limits of Free Speech," by Joyce Arthur, Rewire, September 21, 2011. Reprinted by permission.

origin, gender, sexual orientation, disability, and age), or their occupation, family or marital status, and religion or lack of religion. Proscribing hate speech more broadly would, I believe, foster a more inclusive, tolerant, and safer society.

Many western countries already do criminalize hate speech in a more encompassing way, although enforcement is often weak and spotty. A typical example is Canada, where it is illegal to "expose a person or persons to hatred or contempt…on the basis of a prohibited ground of discrimination" (Canadian Human Rights Act) and to "wilfully promote hatred against any identifiable group" (Criminal Code of Canada). The United States, however, stands almost alone in its veneration of free speech at almost any cost. The U.S. Supreme Court insists that the First Amendment protects hate speech unless it constitutes a "true threat" or will incite imminent lawless action.

But societies should take action against hate speech without requiring that a few specific words by themselves must directly and immediately incite violence, or be likely to. That sets a very high bar and is difficult to prove. It also allows purveyors of hate to evade responsibility simply by not making explicit calls for violence. Further, our new digital world raises the stakes—the Internet has spawned a proliferation of hate speech along with useful information such as bomb-making instructions or the home addresses of abortion providers. This has enabled others to commit violence long after the words were first published.

Violent acts of hate are generally preceded by hate speech that is expressed publicly and repeatedly for years, including by public figures, journalists, leading activists, and even the state. Some examples include Anders Behring Breivik's terrorist acts in Norway (June 2011), the assassination of Kansas abortion provider Dr. George Tiller (May 2009) and other abortion providers in the 1990's, the Rwandan genocide against the Tutsis (1994), the ethnic cleansing of Bosnian Muslims in Bosnia-Herzegovina (1992-1995), and the Nazi Holocaust.

Courts of law should be able to look at broader patterns of hate speech in the culture to determine whether a hateful atmosphere inspired or contributed to violence, or would likely lead to future violence. When hate speech is relatively widespread and acceptable (such as against Muslims or abortion providers), it's not difficult to see the main precursor to violence—an escalation of negative behaviour or rhetoric against the person or group. Dr. George Tiller endured a previous assassination attempt and a decades-long campaign of persecution waged by the anti-abortion movement, which worsened over time, especially in the last year or two of the doctor's life. Anders Behring Breivik had actively opposed multiculturalism for years and had immersed himself in Christian Right propaganda about the supposed threat of Muslim immigration to Europe, a view popularized only in recent years by a growing army of anti-Muslim bloggers and right-wing journalists.

As these examples illustrate, we can often pinpoint the main purveyors of hate speech that lead to violent crimes. In the Norway shootings, the killer Breivik relied heavily on writings from Peder Jensen ("Fjordman"), Pamela Geller, Robert Spencer, Mark Steyn, Jihad Watch, Islam Watch, Front Page Magazine, and others. Such individuals and groups should be charged with incitement to hatred and violence. Similar culpability for the assassination of Dr. George Tiller should rest on the shoulders of the extremist anti-abortion group Operation Rescue and Fox News commentator Bill O'Reilly.

In general, anyone spewing hate to an audience, especially on a repeated basis, could be held criminally responsible. This would include politicians, journalists, organizational leaders and speakers, celebrities, bloggers and hosts of online forums, and radical groups that target certain categories of people. We also need to hold people in accountable positions to a higher standard, such as government employees and contractors, ordained religious leaders, CEOs, and the like.

Criteria by which to assign culpability could include a speaker's past record of prior hate speech against a particular person or group, how widely and frequently the views were disseminated, and the specific content and framing of their views. In cases where violence has already occurred, judges could determine how likely it was that the violent perpetrators had been exposed to someone's specific hate speech, and hand down harsher sentences accordingly.

The Harms of Hate Speech

The apparent assumption of free speech defenders is that offensive speech is essentially harmless—that is, just words with no demonstrable link to consequences. But questioning whether speech can really incite someone to bad behaviour seems irresponsibly obtuse. Obviously, words have consequences and frequently inspire actions. A primary purpose of language is to communicate with others in order to influence them. If that weren't so, there would be no multi-billion-dollar advertising industry, no campaigns for political office, no motivational speakers or books, no citizen-led petitions, no public service announcements, and no church sermons, along with a myriad of other proven examples where speech leads others to act.

The majority of hate speech is targeted towards gays, women, ethnic groups, and religious minorities. It's no coincidence that straight white men are generally the most ardent defenders of near-absolute free speech, because it's very easy to defend hate speech when it doesn't hurt you personally. But hate speech is destructive to the community at large because it is divisive and promotes intolerance and discrimination. It sets the stage for violence by those who take the speaker's message to heart, because it creates an atmosphere of perceived acceptance and impunity for their actions. Left unchecked, it can lead to war and genocide, especially when the state engages in hate speech, such as in Nazi Germany.

Hate speech also has serious effects on its targets. Enduring hatred over many years or a lifetime will take a toll on most people. It can limit their opportunities, push them into poverty, isolate them socially, lead to depression or dysfunction, increase the risk of conflict with authority or police, and endanger their physical health or safety. In 1990, the Canadian Supreme Court stated that hate speech can cause "loss of self-esteem, feelings of anger and outrage and strong pressure to renounce cultural differences that mark them as distinct." The court agreed that "hate propaganda can operate to convince listeners...that members of certain racial or religious groups are inferior," which can increase "acts of discrimination, including the denial of equal opportunity in the provision of goods, services and facilities, and even incidents of violence."

In democratic societies that stand for equality and freedom—often with taxpayer-funded programs that promote those values by assisting vulnerable groups—it makes no sense to tolerate hate speech that actively works to oppose those values. Further, hate speech violates the spirit of human rights codes and laws, diminishing their purpose and effect. A society that allows hate speech is a society that tolerates prejudice at every level—politically, economically, and socially—and pays the consequences through increased discrimination and violence.

Answering Objections from Hate Speech Defenders

The most popular solution to the problem of hate speech is "more free speech." This seems to make sense on the surface, and sometimes works well in practice. For example, there are many outspoken atheists who do a good job of publicly defending themselves and their fellow atheists from the prejudice and hatred too often expressed by religious people. But even if the targets of hatred can ably defend themselves from verbal violence, why should they have to? Why should a democratic society privilege the right to free speech over the well-being and privacy of those with less privilege?

Most vulnerable groups, however, do not have a level playing field on which to respond to hate speech against them. They are often outnumbered, out-resourced, and out-funded by the haters, simply because of their disadvantaged position in society. Sexism and racism are still thriving in the 21st century, which means women and most minority groups have a harder time getting published and heard and taken seriously in mainstream society. Which brings us full circle—perhaps one of the reasons sexism and racism are still so prevalent in modern society is because free speech is exercised largely by the privileged at the expense of the unprivileged.

A common objection to prosecuting hate speech is that it might endanger speech that counters hate speech. For example, a critique may repeat the offending words and discuss their import, or it may subvert the hate message in a subtle or creative way that could be misunderstood by some. But context is everything when determining whether speech is actually hateful or not, so this objection seems nonsensical. Any reasonable judge should be able to discern the difference in intent or effect behind a hateful message and the speech that critiques it.

Another objection is that prosecuting hate speech removes accountability from those who actually commit the violence, turning violent perpetrators into victims of hate speech. But no-one is suggesting that hate speech causes people to act against their will or takes away their personal responsibility. Typically, hate speech creates an environment in which a person who is already sympathetic to the views of the speaker feels validated and encouraged to take action, with a reduced fear of punitive consequences and even anticipation of praise and support from the in-group that shares their views. Nothing prevents a hate-inspired murderer from being prosecuted in the same way as any other violent murderer—in fact, many countries mete out harsher penalties for hate-motivated crimes. But those who inspired the murderer should also be prosecuted separately under hate speech laws.

Many people seem to treat freedom of expression as an almost sacred, inviolable right, but this is far from the reality. In constitutional democracies, free speech is already justifiably restricted in a multitude of ways by law or policy, even in the United States. The quintessential example of prohibited speech is falsely shouting "Fire!" in a crowded theatre. Besides hate speech itself, some other generally accepted prohibitions of speech include:

- Sedition (advocating force as a way to change the government)
- Threats
- Defamation (libel and slander)
- False or misleading advertising
- Buffer zones around abortion clinics that prevent anti-abortion protesters from harassing patients and staff
- Quiet zones near hospitals or schools
- Municipal bylaws restricting the location, size, type, content, and display of signs, posters, objects, ads, etc.
- Profanity on public airwaves
- Publication refusal, censorship, and the right to edit enforced by news websites, online forums and blogs, newspapers, magazines, radio, and other media
- Company confidentiality policies (such as employees being prohibited from sharing trade secrets or talking to the media)
- Gag orders or publication bans in contracts, court cases, and settlements

In practice, courts will look at circumstances on a case-by-case basis to see where a balance should be struck between freedom of expression and some other value or right. No single right trumps another in all circumstances, not even the right to life. For example, Canada's constitution (Section 1 of the Charter of Rights and Freedoms) allows a fundamental right such as freedom of expression to be limited to protect someone else's fundamental rights, such as the right to life or liberty—or in the case of abortion, women's right to safely access a necessary medical service, which courts have determined outweighs the protesters' right to protest outside clinics.

Some current legal restrictions on free speech are not on the above list because they are clearly illegitimate. One of those is insulting your country's head of state, currently illegal in at least eight countries, mostly in western Europe. This offence is called "lese-majesty," a holdover from the days when kings were divine. But if political leaders are immune to criticism or ridicule, they have far too much power over the people and the country cannot be a true democracy. In general, the public must be allowed to pass judgment on public figures, because the latter owe their position to public support in the first place, which should not be coerced or bought. For example, public figures in the U.S. are not protected from defamation unless it was done with malice—knowledge of falsehood or reckless disregard for the truth.

Many countries also criminalize blasphemy—the criticism of religious doctrines or practices. But the desire to protect religion from criticism is simply a reflection of the insecurity of believers who doubt their own beliefs. Blasphemy laws have more in common with hate speech actually, because they often result in hateful rhetoric and violent acts against the "blasphemers." Further, many religious people have a tendency to confuse hate speech with dissent, such as Catholics who hurl accusations of "bigotry" when someone criticizes Church policies or dogma. But hate speech is personal—it is directed against people based on their identifiable characteristics. Dissent on the other hand is speech against other opinions, beliefs, or positions. Dissent is an essential component of a free democracy, and it includes blasphemy. In other words, you should be free to attack Catholic policies that protect abusive priests, but it would be hateful to say that all Catholic priests are pedophiles.

Examples of Anti-Abortion Hate Speech That Should Be Prosecuted

The history of violence against abortion providers makes a very strong case for prosecution of those who disseminate hate speech against them. Almost all of this violence has occurred in the U.S., which makes a compelling argument for limiting First Amendment protections of hate speech.

On a Sunday morning in May 2009, abortion provider Dr. George Tiller was assassinated while attending church in Wichita

Kansas. The killer, Scott Roeder, had been planning the act for some time and had gleaned information about the doctor's movements from Operation Rescue—an anti-abortion group that Roeder was actively involved in and donated money to. This radical group had moved to Wichita in 2002 for the sole purpose of driving Dr. Tiller out of business, and in the seven years leading up to his murder, Operation Rescue (OR) engaged in a relentless campaign of hate and harassment against him, including aggressive picketing, numerous articles and press releases, baseless criminal charges, frivolous lawsuits, and trumped-up grand juries convened against him. (Dr. Tiller was fully vindicated in every legal battle.)

Two years before the assassination, Roeder posted on OR's blog, urging people to attend Dr. Tiller's church. He himself attended the church a few times, and also participated in OR's pickets outside Dr. Tiller's clinic. Roeder was in regular contact with OR's President Troy Newman, as well as Senior Policy Advisor Cheryl Sullenger, who was convicted in 1988 of conspiring to bomb a California abortion clinic. When Roeder was arrested, Sullenger's phone number was found on a post-it note on the dash of his car. Sullenger later admitted having several previous conversations with Roeder, in which she gave him information on Dr. Tiller's habits and whereabouts, including his trial dates. In the months before the murder, Roeder had attended at least one court hearing—sitting beside OR's President Troy Newman—to hear Dr. Tiller defend himself against scurrilous charges brought by OR.

It's clear that Roeder was not a "lone wolf." Perhaps Roeder did not directly involve anyone else in his plans, but no-one develops their views in a vacuum. Dr. Tiller's murder was the natural culmination of over 20 years of anti-abortion harassment and violence directed at him and his clinic, much of it by Operation Rescue. Roeder had been immersed in OR's violent anti-abortion rhetoric for years, so his beliefs and compulsions were fed by that environment, and thrived on it. Obviously, it played an encouraging role in the violence he committed.

Another key person who helped fuel the fire was Fox TV commentator Bill O'Reilly, who has about 3 million listeners. Between 2005 and 2009, Bill O'Reilly and his guest hosts talked about Dr. Tiller on 29 episodes, including just one month before the assassination. The most common epithet repeated many times by O'Reilly was: "Tiller the Baby Killer." Other comments by O'Reilly included: "[Tiller] destroys fetuses for just about any reason right up until the birth date for $5,000." He's guilty of "Nazi stuff." "This is the kind of stuff that happened in Mao's China, Hitler's Germany, Stalin's Soviet Union." He "has blood on his hands." He's "a moral equivalent to NAMBLA and al-Qaida." He operates a "death mill" and a "business of destruction." "I wouldn't want to be [him] if there is a Judgment Day." Although O'Reilly didn't specifically incite someone to murder Dr. Tiller, he put him in the cross-hairs, providing enough motivation and encouragement for someone to carry out the unspoken deed.

Of course, it wasn't just Dr. Tiller and his clinic that were the targets of ongoing harassment and inflammatory hateful rhetoric. The reign of terror directed at clinics and providers across North America has been going on for 35 years—including 9 previous murders and 20 attempted murders of doctors or clinic staff, 100's of arsons and bombs and butyric acid attacks, and 1000's of death threats, stalking, clinic invasions, vandalism, aggressive pickets, and hate mail. Some shootings in the early 1990's were directly preceded by "Wanted Posters" put out by anti-abortion groups on the doctors, complete with their home and clinic addresses and often their photographs. Doctors David Gunn and John Britton were murdered by anti-abortion extremists and had been featured on wanted posters, along with George Tiller, who was shot and wounded in 1993. (The murder of a fourth doctor on a wanted poster, George Patterson, could not be conclusively linked to an anti-abortion extremist.) The posters were deemed by a federal court in 2002 to be a "true threat" under the FACE Act, federal legislation that protects clinics from violence. Noting that the posters had preceded the murders, the court said it was the "use of the 'wanted'-type format in the context of the poster pattern—poster followed by murder—that constitutes the threats," not the language itself. With this decision, the judges overturned a lower court ruling that had deemed the posters and a related website to be "protected speech" because they did not directly threaten violence.

Conclusion

When people and courts defend hate speech against abortion providers as "protected speech," it must be asked: Why are abortion providers required to risk their lives so their persecutors can have free speech rights? Why should doctors constantly have to look over their shoulder in fear, go to work in bullet-proof vests, pay out of pocket for security guards and other expensive safety measures, keep their home address a secret and their curtains permanently drawn shut, and see their children ostracized and bullied at school, just so their persecutors have the right to call them "baby killers"? Why does the right to free speech allow members of this vulnerable minority to be openly defamed and targeted for decades until they're finally assassinated? And why do the families of the slain victims have to suffer in their grief and loss, because free speech was deemed more important than the lives of their loved ones?

The idea that vulnerable persons and groups should have to tolerate hate speech against them in the name of freedom of expression—often over decades or a lifetime—is offensive. We're talking about peoples' lives after all—this is not just a philosophical debate. The right to free speech is a fundamental value, but it should not be allowed to outweigh the basic human rights of other people, especially their right to life.

2

Hate Speech and Free Speech Are Not Relatives

Twigg

Twigg is a lifelong socialist who moved from the United Kingdom to the United States in 2005. Daily Kos is a left-leaning website that supports liberal causes.

Incensed by religious attacks against abortion rights, as well the controversial Westboro Baptist Church — which expresses widely publicized hateful messages against LGBT people and other marginalized groups in American society — this author offers the view that the allowance of hate speech as free speech infringes upon the rights of those targeted. He would prefer to see American youth grow up in a culture in which hate speech, which he equates with bullying and subjugating others, is not tolerated.

One never has to look very far to find those who would cast a baleful eye on any group, any minority, any political or religious belief at variance with their own, and accuse that group of being the ones responsible for damaging the fabric of society, and imperiling the nation.

The *blame game* is a really neat trick if you are dishonest enough to pull it off. It completely absolves you from personal responsibility. No need to examine your own prejudices, attitudes, words or deeds. Freedom from the guilt of a life spent pointing the

"'Hate Speech' is Not the Same as 'Free Speech,'" by Twigg, Kos Media, LLC, August 18, 2013.

finger at your neighbor and, for many, a sure and certain knowledge that you are to leave this Earth for Heaven, because you went to Church every Sunday and never stole, or walked on the cracks in the pavement.

There is one particular group, the Westboro Baptist Church, that serves to demonstrate the perversion of a culture that accepts that not only do we have the right to be judgemental, we also have the right to express our views of others with no regard whatsoever to their well-being; or their right to live free from fear and harassment.

"God Hates Fags". If nothing else there is a simplicity to this message that represents merely the end result of a society where many we consider to be Community Leaders spend an inordinate amount of time thinking about, then preaching about, the sex lives of other people. I am not going to even attempt to pick that appalling phrase apart. Not only is it a complete fail simply on the face of it, it hides multiple fail levels, and fail heaped upon fail should you begin to think about the mindset required to believe it is okay to say things like that. Not only do they say them, they prostrate themselves with them. No, I'm not going to examine it, it is simply a cesspool of depravity.

There was a time when I blamed the 1st Amendment for this ability to spew filth and hatred, regardless of the harm it causes. I have modified that view somewhat, because the Constitution is "just a G'damn piece of paper", no more able to control or modify our behaviour towards each other than the Bible, or the Koran. Those words, never actually confirmed to have been said, but widely attributed to President George Bush sound harsh to many, brought up, as they were, to feel that the Constitution was a document designed and written to form a nation, then guide its future.

The words themselves actually contain a degree of insight that I never credited George Bush with possessing, so I lean towards believing that he didn't actually say them. At least not in the way I believe it to be the truth. As we are seeing in decision after decision, the Supreme Court is and has been playing politics with the Constitution in a manner perhaps not seen since Dred Scott. Bad as this may be, it simply serves to demonstrate that the whole of politics is controlled not by a document, but by people. The decisions are influenced by the words, but the personal thoughts and opinions carry more weight. Justice Scalia is quite capable of reversing himself from one case to the next, this is not news.

It's not the written word that permits the outpouring of hatred from the Westboro Baptists or any number of White Supremacist groups, it is our society's propensity to tolerate them. The written word can inform. In some circumstances, it can guide the actions of others. What it cannot do is change behavior in a country, and among a people who may find such behaviour repugnant, yet seem to feel that these groups have the right to speak freely. Often my suspicion is that much of the hate is not very far removed from many of the thoughts of those in polite society. Although they might be too refined to utter the words themselves, neither are they minded to actually condemn with positive actions, those of others.

I sometimes wonder how we will ever prevent the youth, in our schools and colleges, parks and playgrounds, from verbally abusing gay, lesbian, black, brown, disabled and any other minority, when the adults tell them we have a right to free speech, and they can see for themselves the Westboro Baptists holding their disgusting placards. When they can see and hear the filth spewed by good, God-fearin' Christians outside Women's Health Clinics. We know they are "God-fearin'", because they tell us so. Apparently, the bit about "love thy neighbor" somehow was lost in translation.

Of course, it is simply wrong. No one has the right to behave in this manner, even if the laws appear to permit it. There is no such thing as unfettered free speech, we simply haven't fettered the right bits yet. We have not yet matured sufficiently as a society to codify the very simple principle that your rights extend only to the point where they infringe upon the rights of others, and not one inch further. We have reached the point where it is unacceptable to discriminate against some minority groups in housing, employment and a raft of other areas, yet the nuance is missing.

We still allow *hate speech*, we still allow discrimination against LGBT people in very many areas. We do not recognize those people as citizens with full rights, the pursuit of happiness among them, because we still allow and support the idea that others are free to impinge upon that happiness, and make the lives of others as miserable as they can. We protect that position with the supreme law of the land. We talk about Right to Work as if it is an employment matter. We justify it by suggesting that employers must be flexible, that they might create a maximum number of jobs. We fail to push back against Right to Work with the most powerful argument we have; that Right to Work is effectively a rolling back of generations of hard-won civil rights. You can't fire workers for being black, or Muslim, or Jewish, but you can fire them, or discriminate in hiring, if you are able to fire for no reason. See what they did there?

The people of the United States generally hold the view that they live in the world's greatest country, and the world's greatest democratic republic. Well I wouldn't argue with the first bit. I think everyone should feel a certain pride in their community and country. I'm torn, because I'm not American and even I feel some pride in your country. I'm far less sure about the second part though.

It is some perverse irony, given the current political landscape, that it was Abraham Lincoln, a Republican, who uttered these words:

"But, in a larger sense, we cannot dedicate -- we cannot consecrate -- we cannot hallow -- this ground. The brave men, living and dead, who struggled here, have consecrated it, far above our poor power to add or detract. The world will little note, nor long remember what we say here, but it can never forget what they did here. It is for us the living, rather, to be dedicated here to the unfinished work which they who fought here have thus far so nobly advanced. It is rather for us to be here dedicated to the great task remaining before us -- that from these honored dead we take increased devotion to that cause for which they gave the last full measure of devotion -- that we here highly resolve that these dead shall not have died in vain -- that this nation, under God, shall have a new birth of freedom -- and that government of the people, by the people, for the people, shall not perish from the earth."

Yet when I look around the developed world, it seems that the people have fewer advantages here than in most other countries. It seems that America is the one country among a raft of comparable societies that has done the least for its people, yet many of the people think it has done the most.

Pick an area .... Employment rights, Trades Union rights, Pension provision, Sick Leave, Parental leave, ANY leave. Minimum wage, the right to healthcare, Education provision. The right to legal redress and a humane justice system. The rights of minorities, women, gays.

Point to any of those areas and explain how Americans have more rights, or better provision than any European nation .... Even the other North American nation seems to be managing its affairs more equitably.

We are terrific at making laws that jail folk for personal drug use, but the Holocaust Deniers are walking the streets, publishing their Blogs, Tweeting their filth and generally going unhindered about their business. It is curious that a habit that mostly affects only an individual is illegal, and one that seeks to subjugate and torment the lives of others is protected. Something is deeply flawed about that.

We need to be smarter, and I know many of my readers are just that. We need to be smarter as a society. We need to start putting people first, and we could consider that the judgemental behaviour of a large section of our society is not just hampering our development; it is a self-fulfilling prophesy. If we allow the fundamentalists to spread poverty and hatred, then we create whole sections of society that has little of value, and less to value. Then we point to those sectors and complain that they commit most of the crime. At the very same time, we allow others who commit far more serious crimes to appear on Talk Shows, blaming the criminals. It's a sweet system we have going.

There will be those who will tell me that we can't outlaw speech. That the thought police have no place in our country, that we have freedoms! Well if we are going down that road, I will simply respond by saying that the day that "God Hates Fags" on a placard, becomes illegal; then that is a day I will celebrate. Why shouldn't it be illegal? The day that those we elect to be judges begin to deal harshly with the worst expressions of the judgemental is a day that cannot come quickly enough. Not because I want to see any stifling of debate. Not because I would think it a good idea to outlaw different views and opinions, but because the term "Free Speech" carries a responsibility, which is to use your freedoms wisely. They are not an excuse to subjugate others, and we should not be tolerating it.

**

After I had finished writing this Diary I came across a story that typifies the kind of hate speech that concerns me the most.

It is a story from Portland, Oregon, and is reminiscent of the outing of abortion providors, a campaign that led directly to the murder of at least one doctor.

In this instance, an anonymous coward calling themselves Artemis of the Woodland has circulated a flyer threatening to "name and shame" people on disability in a Portland neighborhood.

Later I found a Diary on the subject by Cartoon Peril. The whole episode is clearly designed to be hateful, and to intimidate people who are already suffering, because scapegoating is easy, and the disabled are not to be taken to the waters at Lourdes and cured, but shamed.

In that Diary, the commenters were clear that this odious communication probably strayed right up to the line of legality, but stayed the right side. Yet clearly the message was designed to strike fear through intimidation. It is hate speech, pure and simple.

All of this is bad enough, yet could be put down to a single warped individual who should be in jail, but probably won't be found .... Except he might be, by this guy who I found in the Portland personals of Craigslist:

Artemis of the Wildland

Looks like you're under some scrutiny. But I see what you're trying to do, and I like the creative problem solving.

We should talk, we would make good associates.

The link might not stay up, so I copied the message here. Whoever this person is, he (and it is almost always a "he"), heard of the story and wishes to expand on the domestic terrorism represented by this nasty campaign of hatred.

It might be that the law simply can't make the definition. It's like pornography ... I can't describe it but I know it when I see it. If that is correct, then maybe we should have a broad law that criminalizes hate speech, and we can let the courts "know it when they see it", and set the boundaries accordingly.

If we fail to act decisively, to protect those who we know are vulnerable, and who are being targeted for intimidation, then I am wholly unsure why those people should not simply believe that we as a society support this kind of abuse.

***

10:37 AM PT: Before there are many more comments about "loving" the 1st Amendment, I would like to remind the demographic of this Blog of a few pertinent issues.

This is NOT an academic argument. These points, as they relate to hate speech, are not an arcane discussion about rights and freedoms.

I don't know where you all live, but in areas of America where the hate is palpable, these are real problems, for real people. The hate and bullying are real, they affect real lives.

Not outlawing any speech might satisfy your inner liberal, but it does not help when we signally fail to send a powerful message to those who use their "rights" to bully, harass and subjugate.

3

Harmless Hate? There's No Such Thing

Jeremy Waldron

Jeremy Waldron teaches legal and political philosophy at the New York University School of Law. He has written extensively on issues such as democracy, homelessness, and the Constitution. Waldron has also authored a book titled The Harm of Hate Speech (2012).

The author of this piece stresses that those who equate hate speech with free speech and argue against its prohibition tend to underrate the harm it causes. He claims that legislation, where it exists, barring hate speech has brought a sense of dignity to the societies it seeks to protect. The belief is that the potential for public good outweighs any possible benefits of unrestricted freedom of speech.

"We speak openly and with civility about all kinds of human difference" is the fourth draft principle for global free expression proposed by the Free Speech Debate project. That is something we can all applaud. But as Timothy Garton Ash's commentary indicates, it raises further issues that are not conveyed in the formulation of the principle itself. Should "speaking openly" mean speaking without any legal constraint, even when the speech is manifestly uncivil? So the discussion raises the issue of hate speech and the difficult question about whether it is ever appropriate to legislate against it.

"The Harm of Hate Speech", by Jeremy Waldron, Eurozine, April 24, 2012. Reprinted by permission.

The most striking thing about Timothy's commentary on this issue is the absence of any substantial consideration of the harm that hate speech may do to those who are its targets. The message conveyed by a hateful pamphlet or poster, attacking someone on grounds of race, religion, sexuality, or ethnicity, is something like this:

"Don't be fooled into thinking you are welcome here. The society around you may seem hospitable and non-discriminatory, but the truth is that you are not wanted, and you and your families will be shunned, excluded, beaten, and driven out, whenever we can get away with it. We may have to keep a low profile right now. But don't get too comfortable. Remember what has happened to you and your kind in the past. Be afraid."

That message is conveyed viciously and publicly. To the extent that they can, the purveyors of this hate will try to make it a visible and permanent feature of our social fabric. And members of the vulnerable groups targeted are expected to live their lives, conduct their business, raise their children, and allay their nightmares in a social atmosphere poisoned by this sort of speech.

Not only that, but the aim of this sort of speech is to defame the members of the vulnerable groups in question — to do whatever they can do to lower their reputation in the eyes of others and to make it as difficult as possible for them to engage in ordinary social interactions.

As I understand it, Timothy's position is that the civil authorities should have no interest in this at all, no concern about the impact of on the lives of those who are targeted by hate speech. His discussion shows this by not dwelling on the effect or impact of hate speech and by implying that anyone who does dwell on the harm that may be done by hate speech is, for that reason alone, an enemy of freedom of expression.

A case can perhaps be made that legislation on these matters is chilling and counter-productive. We certainly need to discuss that. (Actually, I don't accept the speculative "slippery slope" reasoning conveyed in Timothy's commentary of Principle 4, but I do accept that there are serious questions to be addressed.) However, no discussion of the free speech/hate speech issue can possibly be taken seriously if it does not consider the harm that those who advocate the regulation of hate speech are trying to address.

So: what I would most like to see added to our discussion of Principle 4 is some consideration of this harm — I mean consideration at length, not just shrugged off in a line or two — and some explicit attempt to defend the position, which I think is implicit in the existing discussion, that the harm of hate speech pales into insignificance compared to the chilling effect of any legislation on the speakers themselves.

Once we understand the harm that hate speech may inflict, we are in a better position to grasp the argument in favour of the legislation that restricts it. Such legislation, in the countries where it exists, aims to uphold important elements of basic social order — and in particular the civic status or basic dignity of all who live in the society. Particularly in communities with histories of injustice or in modern conditions of religious or ethnic diversity, one cannot assume that the basic dignitary order will be upheld. There will always be attempts to stigmatise, marginalise, intimidate, or exclude members of distinct and vulnerable groups, and what we call hate speech is often a way of doing this or initiating this. As I have argued in "Dignity and Defamation: The Visibility of Hate" (the 2009 Holmes Lectures at Harvard University), hate speech legislation seeks to uphold a public good by protecting the basic dignitary order of society against this kind of attack.

Legislative attention to hate speech is like environmental legislation; it seeks to preserve a very elementary aspect of the social environment against both sudden and slow-acting poisons of a particularly virulent kind. Of course, we hope that attempts to underline the social order will be met with strong responses that are, equally, exercises of free speech. But legislation may be necessary, because there is no guarantee (and it is little short of superstitious to think that there is a guarantee) that more speech is an effective answer to hate speech.

Such legislation needs to be drafted with care. It needs to distinguish, for example, between attacks on people's basic dignity and reputation, and attacks on their beliefs (the former are appropriate topics for legislative concern, but not the latter). It also needs to define alternative ways — non-virulent ways — of expressing the substance of the concerns that people may have about the behaviour of other groups or members in society, ways that will not attract legal sanctions. The best hate speech legislation takes care to do this. Its aim is to confine the application of legal sanctions to speech-acts, which directly and deliberately seek to make it impossible for their targets to live lives of basic dignity in our society.

4

Hate Speech Is Risky Business

Devin Foley

Devin Foley is the co-founder and president of Intellectual Takeout, a digital media non-profit that serves to spur political debate. He previously served as director of development at the Center of the American Experiment, a state-based think tank in Minnesota.

In this article, the author argues that — just as what is considered offensive to one person might not be to another — the definition of hate speech can also be construed differently by a variety of hearts and minds. He therefore contends that banning perceived hate speech places society on a slippery slope. Banning hate speech, he says, should be resisted with as much force as possible.

Russell Kirk argued that to engage in politics and ideas we must "draw the sword of imagination." By that he meant, we must imagine all the ways in which a policy or an idea may do either good or harm.

Recently, Facebook, Twitter, and other social media giants announced that they will be working with the European Union (EU) to censor "hate speech".

> Under the terms of a code of conduct, the firms, which also include YouTube and Microsoft, have committed to 'quickly and efficiently' tackle illegal hate speech directed against anyone over issues of race, color, religion, descent or national or ethnic

"The Dangers of 'Hate Speech' Rules," by Devin Foley, Intellectual Takeout, June 2, 2016. Reprinted by permission.

origin. The sites have often been used by terrorist organizations to relay messages and entice hatred against certain individuals or groups.

Among the measures agreed with the EU's executive arm, the firms have said they will establish internal procedures and staff training to guarantee that a majority of illegal content is assessed and, where necessary, removed within 24 hours. They have also agreed to strengthen their partnerships with civil society organizations who often flag content that promotes incitement to violence and hateful conduct. The European Commission and the firms have also agreed to support civil society organizations to deliver 'anti-hate campaigns.'

'The internet is a place for free speech, not hate speech,' said Vera Jourova, the EU commissioner responsible for justice, consumers and gender equality.

The danger in such a pronouncement is that what is free speech to one person is considered hate speech by another. Either you have free speech or you do not.

In America, we have a long history of legal debate over the term "free speech" and what the government may or may not suppress. Over time, we have kept our tradition alive while also recognizing that some speech does not qualify for protection. Things like death threats, incitements to violence, and libel aren't covered, but overall we are quite lenient. Additionally, of course, private companies like Facebook and Twitter have every right to censor speech on their property.

Freedom of speech is a fairly easy concept to wrap one's mind around. If a person wants to speak out on a topic that is or should be of concern to the public, he has every right to do so even if the majority of people disagree with him. But what about the term "hate speech"?

First of all, without Googling it, can you define it? Not so easily, right?

Here's what the American Civil Liberties Union (ACLU) has to say about it:

Many universities, under pressure to respond to the concerns of those who are the objects of hate, have adopted codes or policies prohibiting speech that offends any group based on race, gender, ethnicity, religion or sexual orientation.

If you've drawn your sword of imagination, that definition should alarm you the most because of the word "offend". The possibilities for abuse should be more than obvious. Under such a definition, if you say something that I don't like, I can appeal to the authorities on the grounds that you offended me and I am, therefore, a victim of hate speech. Depending on who you are and who I am, the authorities may punish you severely for offending me. If I am a "protected class" listed in the definition, I have enormous power to censor your speech based on my emotional reaction.

At Ball State University, we find another definition of hate speech:

Hate speech consists of verbal and nonverbal expression that is used to demean, oppress, or promote violence against someone on the basis of their membership in a social or ethnic group. Hate speech involves more than simply indicating that you dislike someone. It also is different than simply teasing or ridiculing someone, or shouting an ugly word at them in a single moment of anger or frustration.

In many cases, hate speech is created by people who are part of a majority population. Their messages typically are directed toward people who are part of a minority population. The targets of hate speech are chosen just because they belong to that particular group of people. The messages of hate also are designed to degrade or otherwise harm these targets for the same reason.

The Ball State University definition gets a lot murkier and even more open to abuse. While one may argue that it is good to stop speech that promotes violence against others, that assumes we're working with the traditional definition of violence, something we don't know from the description. As of late, it's become popular to claim that hurtful or offensive words are a form of violence in and of themselves. We can see the argument manifested in a student editorial in The Harvard Crimson:

> When someone calls a black person the 'n' word out of hatred, he or she is not expressing a new idea or outlining a valuable thought. They are committing an act of violence. Speech has great power. It can—and often does—serve as a tool to marginalize and oppress people. Laws that restrict hate speech simply seek to prevent violence against marginalized, oppressed groups in order to prevent them from becoming further marginalized and oppressed.

The student further expands upon this idea:

> There are freedoms to do things, and there are freedoms from things. When our freedom to speak our mind impinges on someone's freedom from fear, or on someone's right to feel safe in their community, then that freedom should not stand unregulated in any group that wishes to create a safe and respectful society for its members. We cannot create a respectful learning environment at our university if students from marginalized groups feel that their administration condones acts of violence against them. University regulations against hate speech are entirely necessary for maintaining respect and dignity among the student body, and Harvard's policies to this end are well thought-out and fair—and certainly not worthy of protest.

Making offensive speech the equivalent of physical violence is a very dangerous road to go down. In doing so, we effectively eliminate the meaning of words as well as the ability to have a tough, but logical conversation. Everything comes down to feelings and whether or not a person is in a protected class.

The idea of free speech is that you have the right to say something no matter if the majority of people are with you or against you. What happens under hate speech rules is quite the opposite. A minority, even just one person, has the power to shut down all speech that he finds offensive as long as the authorities are of a similar mind and the individual is part of a protected class.

You cannot have free speech if you have hate speech regulations. As the ACLU argues:

> The First Amendment to the United States Constitution protects speech no matter how offensive its content. Speech codes adopted by government-financed state colleges and universities amount to government censorship, in violation of the Constitution. And the ACLU believes that all campuses should adhere to First Amendment principles because academic freedom is a bedrock of education in a free society.
>
> How much we value the right of free speech is put to its severest test when the speaker is someone we disagree with most. Speech that deeply offends our morality or is hostile to our way of life warrants the same constitutional protection as other speech because the right of free speech is indivisible: When one of us is denied this right, all of us are denied. Since its founding in 1920, the ACLU has fought for the free expression of all ideas, popular or unpopular. That's the constitutional mandate.

On this point, the ACLU is absolutely correct. The constitutional mandate is to protect all speech, not just culturally accepted speech. Furthermore, the push to control speech on college campuses and other public spaces should be met with the fiercest resistance possible.

And while Facebook and Twitter have every right to control speech on their private platforms, they should be very, very careful when censoring content as they've arguably put themselves out there as platforms for public discourse. If not, then we can only hope competitors to the social media giants come online soon otherwise public discourse in America and around the world will be severely restrained with the public reaction unpredictable.

5

Free Speech Seems to Be Selective

Raouf Halaby

Raouf Halaby is a writer and English and art teacher who has been awarded Professor Emeritus status at Ouachita Baptist University in Arkadelphia, Arkansas. Counterpunch is an intellectual online and print magazine that touts itself as a "fearless muckraking" publisher established in 1993.

Inspired by events in Europe and the Middle East, the author warns against the inconsistencies of defining free speech and hate speech, specifically in regard to religion, but also concerning other issues. Halaby argues that such inconsistencies allow hate to spread, leading to violence and then counter-violence. He stresses that the American government must side with the righteous rather than the corrupt and adds that only through diplomacy and well-intentioned discussion can issues between people be resolved peacefully.

E ven though the details about the producer of a 13-minute film about the life of the Prophet Muhammad are vague, the film has ignited a firestorm of protests and anger in North Africa, the Near East, and Central Asia. Alleged to be a Los Angeles Copt of Egyptian background, Sam Bacile (believed to be an alias for Nakoula Bassily Nakoula) has produced a despicable film that has not only drawn on every imaginable Muslim stereotype, but it has

"The Cycle of Hate, Anger, Violence and Counter-Violence," by Raouf Halaby, Counterpunch, September 17, 2012. Reprinted by permission. Originally appeared on CounterPunch.org, September 17, 2012.

also indulged in hate speech and the vilification of the youngest of the Abrahamic faiths.

In a series of disjointed and non-sequential scenes and through an assortment of bizarre characters who interact with the Prophet Bacile's first scene establishes the following: The Prophet has 61 wives and girlfriends; he is depicted as a disheveled Neanderthal; he is sitting outside a tent in a desert-like setting; he is wildly grasping onto a large bone, wolfing down large chunks of stringy meat; and he is repeatedly described as a bastard. In the second scene, the Prophet is asked to go into a tent where a seated woman (with widespread legs and thighs completely exposed) who first tells him that, because he has no underwear, he needs to be modest. Soon she [directs him to perform a sexual act on her,] something he lasciviously obliges.

To enhance the negative stereotype, a series of close-ups and cropped scenes depict Muslims in the vilest manner. They have ugly teeth, long, stringy beards, their robes are filthy; they brandish bloody swords in every scene, they sell children into slavery so as to buy weapons, they are good at looting, and threaten their captives with "extortion or death;" they claim that "every non-Muslim is an infidel" and their "lands, their women, their children are our spoils." The Prophet is portrayed as "a child molester," a gay man, "a murderous thug," and a lascivious character who "forces himself on women." In the last few scenes the Prophet is represented as a serial sex fiend/rapist who derives pleasure from seeing an old woman whose legs are torn asunder by two camels walking in opposite directions. For a virulently racist finale, the final scene depicts the execution of a young captive tied to a pole – a sword dripping with blood is shown behind the man's back and above his head.

Last week the reaction in the Muslim world was swift, bloody, and very messy. From Morocco, North Africa's most Western Muslim country, to Sudan, Egypt, Iraq and as far as Central Asia, Muslims have reacted with fury. And, ironically, in Tunisia and Egypt, two so-called Arab Springers, the US embassies were attacked and firebombed. The unkindest cut of all occurred in Libya, a country the Obillary/Sarkozy/Cameron/Merkel/Berlusconi team bombed into yet another iffy Arab Spring; cowardly revenge was exacted on four innocent American men. Sarkozy lost his re-election bid and Obama, in a fight for his re-election, sent two naval ships to Libya.

The heinous killing of US Ambassador Christopher Stephens and embassy employees Glen Doherty, Sean Smith, and Tyrone Woods is a barbaric crime that should be criticized by everyone, especially folks in the Arab world. So should the slaughter of tens of thousands of Arab civilians.

The abhorrent and cold-blooded murder is a blatant violation of Bedouin/Arab codes that predate Islam and are enshrined in the Arab and Muslim traditions; these codes have been revered and practiced for centuries. Generosity and hospitality are valued and honored as sacrosanct social norms of conduct that govern one's interactions with family, friends, guests and the extended community. This code stipulates that a guest, even a stranger, must be honored, respected, and protected. By committing this dastardly deed, the killers have not only committed an egregious crime and violated a sacred code, but they have also helped reinforce all the negative stereotypes and myths that have become a well-organized and well-funded cottage industry of virulent anti-Muslim xenophobia in the U.S. and Europe. Politicians, self-styled preachers, pundits, and pseudo scholars have exploited the 9/11 tragedy to promote their agendas. And all the recent rhetorical platitudes about the Arab Spring are phony; pandering politicians and partisan pundits, and especially a media that has gone AWOL, have clearly demonstrated that they have a superficial understanding of the root causes of the deep resentment the Arab and Muslim worlds harbor towards the West. And a failed Obillary Drone/capitulation-to-Netanyahu and a cozy friendship with the Dictators-for-Life Arab potentates approach to the current failed Foreign Policy have not helped. And God help us if the trigger-happy Mitt/Ryan team is elected come November.

From Morocco to the west and as far as Bangladesh to the east, indigenous populations harbor deep resentment towards British, French, and Italian colonial rule, a domination that was characterized by brutal suppression; for well over a century now exploiting the natural resources and geo-strategic control trumped everything. The post 1917 dicing, slicing and redrawing of geographical boundaries by Britain and France (especially in Palestine, Greater Syria, Turkey, Kurdistan, Iraq and Pakistan) without regard to historic, national and ethic sensitivities was a serious mistake for which the region and the rest of the world are paying even to this day; Palestine, Lebanon, Syria, Kurdistan, and Iraq have borne the brunt of this meddling. Since the early 1950's North Africa and the Near East have exchanged the European tyrannical yokes for equally brutal indigenous tyrannical yokes. Many of today's tyrants hide behind religion and the Palestinian Nakba to suppress their populations. And since the 1950's the peoples of the region have been living under the tyranny of two yokes; regional dictators and their western oil-addicted bedfellows have struck a Faustian compact to maintain a steady flow of the black gold.

When Mel Gibson's film *The Passion of the Christ* was released in 2004, many in the Christian community voiced their disbelief and anger at what they perceived to be an affront to Christianity, and leading Jewish organizations voiced their concerns about the age-old libel charge. In his collage The Holy Virgin Mary, Chris Ofili mixed elephant dung and dead animals to create an image of the Virgin, a medium that elicited a very strong reaction by leading Catholic figures. Rudy Giuliani 's 1999 attempts to punish (funding and legal proceedings) the Brooklyn Art Museum ended in a draw. Mapplethorpe's all too explicitly homoerotic photographs were lambasted, and attempts to prosecute the Cincinnati Contemporary Art Center failed. Piss Christ, a 1987 photograph by Andrea Serrano, raised the ire of Christians, especially Catholics, and politicians. The artist placed a plastic crucifix in a vial containing his urine; Jessie Helms threatened to withhold funding from the

National Endowment for the Arts. Free speech won the day for Ofili and Serrano. However, Serrano's photograph was met with stronger reactions in other climes; in Australia the photograph was vandalized, and on Palm Sunday 2011 angry protesters forced their way into a gallery in Avignon, France, and destroyed the composition with hammers. In his re-election bid for the French presidency, Sarkozy attempted to make political hay by siding with the demonstrators.

In 2004 film maker, writer and critic Theo van Gogh collaborated with Somali-born Dutch citizen Ayan Hirsi to produce an eleven-minute film under the title Submission. Instead of producing a statement on the status of women in Muslim societies, the film employed some of the worst Muslim and Arab stock stereotyping that included a scene on arranged marriages, a scene on the flogging of women, and a pernicious scene on the molestation of a girl by a relative. The scenes were presented as routine denigration and molestation of women in Muslim societies. It is analogous to judging American society by the reprehensible child molestation of children by Catholic priests and the likes of Jerry Sandusky? Prior to the film's release, Van Gogh's anti-immigrant sentiments had been duly noted in print and public forums. In late 2004 Van Gogh was senselessly murdered by a Dutch Moroccan, and in November of that year there were 106 anti-Muslim retaliatory attacks on mosques and Muslims in Holland. Subsequent parliamentary discussions on blasphemy laws (against Jews, Christians and Muslims) got nowhere.

In 2005 the Danish newspaper Jyllands–Politiken published several cartoons depicting the Prophet Muhammad in less than flattering terms, and one cartoon in particular depicted the Prophet with a turban in the shape of a bomb. At the same time the newspaper refused to publish anti-Christian and anti-Jewish cartoons drawn by Danish artists. Demonstrations and protests in Denmark and across Europe and the Middle East (some of which turned violent and bloody) hardened European resolve and German, Swedish, French and Belgian newspapers printed the same cartoons. And threats of economic boycotts of Danish goods prompted Danish Prime Minister Anders Rasmussen to state that this was Denmark's worst crisis since WWII. I am of the opinion that the fault lines in Europe's economic woes were by then becoming more apparent, and the tendency to use immigrants as scapegoats for economic problems added fuel to the xenophobic sentiments that had begun to sweep through Europe. This, combined with violent demonstrations in Europe and the Muslim worlds, served as a wedge issue in what can be best described as the new cultural wars. Because Muslim immigrants, by and large, are concentrated in ghettoized neighborhoods, the process of assimilation (through education and employment) in the fabric of European societies is slow. Marginalized economically, socially and politically, and told (through legislation) that their women could not wear the traditional head scarves, European Muslims, angry, alienated, and having the welcome rug pulled from under their feet, have found solace and comforting affinities in the social and religious support they find in their own ethnic enclaves, the Little Pakistans, Little Moroccos, and Little Iraqs.

While free speech won the day in Denmark and across Europe, it did nothing to mend the fault line of mistrust that has alienated white Europeans and their Muslim minorities. Many Muslims rightfully have posed the following question: Why is it that many European countries have passed laws prohibiting anyone from denying the Holocaust — even to the extent of prosecuting and imprisoning those who utter the rabid denial? And why are public figures and the media allowed to denigrate the Prophet and Islam by resorting to virulent images and hateful narratives? Why is one prosecuted for voicing an opinion and the other given a pass under the guise and protection of free speech? Are the two not equally abhorrent? And finally, why is it that the European Forum on Anti-Semitism has remained silent when the religion of millions of Semitic Muslims is vilified?

Those who think that military might and billion-dollar bribes in the form of foreign aid are going to change the deep-seated resentment towards the US and the West are wrong. Besides, we've seen the poor return on the military adventures in Iraq, Afghanistan, and Libya, and how the foreign aid with which we, the taxpayers of this country entrust our leaders, goes into tyrants' Swiss accounts and regional military adventures.

George Bush's answer to his own question about "Why do they hate us?" was answered with a bloody war that pulverized Iraq back to the stone age and brought us to the brink of financial disaster. It would take several volumes to expound on "Why do they hate us?" To put it succinctly, the digital technology has pulled the drape on two sore spots that feed into the anguish and humiliation that plague the Muslim and Arab worlds. And it is through these two prisms that the Muslim masses filter regional and international events and policies.

In Israel and the occupied territories mosques and Korans are burned and defiled, Muslim cemeteries are bulldozed (as in the case of the 7th century Mamila cemetery which was leveled and over 7,000 thousand graves were desecrated and dug up so as to build, of all things, a Simon Wiesenthal Center of Tolerance). Palestinians are being ethnically cleansed in a perniciously systematic peristaltic manner, and natural resources are stolen from their rightful owners. Only two weeks ago, Jewish settlers broke into the compound of a Catholic monastery and defaced the walls with graffiti; "Jesus is a monkey" said one phrase. To their credit, a handful of Israelis apologized and made amends. That Netanyahu is holding Obama, Romney, and the US Congress at bay, and that he is weekly threatening to bomb Iran leaves the folks in that region of the world in fear of yet another senseless war, and it seems to me that these violent reactions should also be seen as a painful cry by the masses of the region: We're tired of war!!! Enough is enough, not in my neighborhood, not no more.

The second and equally important prism has to do with a fractious Arab world of haves and have nots, both of which are ruled by corrupt tyrants. Muslim Malaysian, Bangladeshi, and Indonesian nationals who toil in indentured servitude in the oil rich Gulf countries resent the manner in which they are treated. And the sloshy oil rich rulers are expending fortunes to stay in power. And because of the West's insatiable addiction to oil, these potentates muscle Washington into abeyance. In a quid pro quo clutch they've become surrogates for military intervention (Libya and Syria are cases in point); how ironic, while Saudi Arabia and Qatar have supported the Libyan uprisings, they have denied the minorities in their midst the same freedom. And finally, there is a history of brutal assaults etched in the minds of Near Easterners. The British meddling in Iran and Iraq which dates to the 1920's when Churchill dropped ton after ton of mustard gas on Iraqi civilians, a violation that was repeated with guided missiles in the last decade during which tens of thousands of Iraqi civilians were killed, maimed, or humiliated in the infamous Abu Ghreibs that sprouted in Iraq and Afghanistan. And there are lingering memories of US outsourced torture in Egypt, Syria, and Jordan. One can only hope that should Obama get re-elected, he would change the course of US foreign policy. We need to make friends with the masses, and not those who rule them.

By all accounts Ambassador Stephens loved the people of the region. He spoke their language, he understood their culture, and he was trying to help Libyans forge their way out of chaos and into a democratic future. He was a guest in Libya, and he should have been treated as such and accorded protection.

Is it not time for sane Jews, sane Christians, and sane Muslims to sit down for a serious discussion about peace and harmony?

6

Education Depends on Free Speech, Even Hate Speech

Greg Lukianoff

Greg Lukianoff is an attorney and president and CEO of the Foundation for Individual Rights in Education (FIRE). He has also authored books about campus censorship and freedom from speech and co-authored a guide to free speech on campus.

The following piece is a plea to universities to not only educate students about the subjects they study, but also about the value of free speech to American society. The author opines that, based on the success students have had in recent years stifling speakers with whom they do not agree, schools have not done their due diligence in teaching the importance of allowing all sides of issues to be expressed. He believes that only when all views are accepted can we as a nation live up to our ideals in regard to free speech.

For those of you who are concerned about the state of free expression on campus, I would like to introduce you to Texas Tech University's "Free Speech Gazebo." The Gazebo is only 20 feet wide, and in early 2003, it was the sole area on campus where students could engage in free-speech activities — demonstrations, speeches or even handing out pamphlets — without clearing it with the university a minimum of six days in advance.

"Colleges Must Educate Students About Value of Free Speech," by Greg Lukianoff, Foundation for Individual Rights in Education, December 29, 2004. Reprinted by permission.

To illustrate the lunacy of this policy, I asked one of my friends, who has a math degree from MIT, how tightly you would have to pack the Free Speech Gazebo in order to fit all of Texas Tech's 28,000 students. He deduced that, if (God forbid) all Texas Tech students wanted to exercise their free-speech rights at the same time, you would have to crush them down to the density of Uranium 238.

Unsatisfied with 280 square feet of freedom, Texas Tech student Trevor Smith contacted the Foundation for Individual Rights in Education. Smith and his group, Students for Social Justice, wanted to hold a protest against the Bush administration's policies toward Iraq. Texas Tech officials told Smith that the protest would be allowed only in the gazebo.

On Feb. 6, 2003, one day before the protest, the foundation wrote to Donald R. Haragan, president of Texas Tech, urging him to respect his students' rights. The next day, the students held their planned protest outside of the gazebo without interference from the administration.

Yet, despite promises to greatly expand the area designated for speech, Texas Tech's speech-zone policy remained, along with a clearly unconstitutional speech code. So on July 12, 2003, the foundation and the Alliance Defense Fund launched a legal challenge against Tech's speech polices.

Earlier this fall, the U.S. District Court for the Northern District of Texas threw out much of Texas's speech code as unconstitutional and ruled that the policy must be interpreted to allow free speech for students on "park areas, sidewalks, streets, or other similar common areas ... irrespective of whether the University has so designated them or not."

While banishing free speech to a gazebo may seem almost funny, this lack of respect for free expression at institutions that rely on openness and debate to function properly is no laughing matter. Speech codes that ban "offensive" speech, and speech zone policies that quarantine expression to tiny areas of campus, teach students that free speech is at best a joke and at worst a nuisance to be done away with by any means necessary.

And students have been learning these lessons well for years now. In the spring of 2002, a New York Times article headlined "Debate? Dissent? Don't Go There!" explored the growing perception that modern college students are more guarded about their views than students of previous generations. The author reviewed a number of potential causes for this, including the unifying effect of Sept. 11, disgust with partisan politics, the uncivil debates students see on cable news programs and simple politeness. Curiously absent from this article, however, was any suggestion that they may be learning this attitude from the colleges themselves.

Today's students are doubtless aware that speech which offends anyone can get them in serious trouble. Just this year, at universities including University of Massachusetts at Amherst, Occidental College, Rhode Island College, George Washington University, University of Georgia, and University of New Hampshire, students and faculty who engaged in what would be protected speech in the larger society were evicted from housing, suspended, sentenced to mandatory psychological counseling, threatened with expulsion, and found guilty of serious offenses ranging from "harassment" to "disorderly conduct."

The phenomenon of "free speech areas" perhaps best represents the attitude toward free speech at many colleges and universities today. Free expression will be tolerated but only grudgingly and only when it is agreeable, tightly controlled and regulated. Dozens, possibly hundreds, of schools mandate tiny, restrictive speech zones. In the past few years, we have received reports of unconstitutional speech zones at Clemson University, Western Illinois University, Florida State University, University of Nebraska at Omaha, University of Oregon, Ithaca College, California State University at Chico, West Virginia University, and University of Northern Texas, just to name a handful.

With so many schools propagating rules that are hostile to freely following expression, where exactly are students supposed to learn to value freedom of speech? They will not learn it in their classes, as the Times article made clear, and they are not likely to learn it in their student activities, which are tightly regulated and controlled. They are even unlikely to learn respect for free speech from their fellow students.

If the continuing problem of students stealing - and often destroying - newspapers to repress opinions and articles they dislike is any indication (an all too common and well-documented form of grass-roots censorship that most recently reared its ugly head at Yale University), free speech faces an uncertain future. Under these circumstances, we shouldn't be surprised when college students think twice about opening their mouths.

For the sake of the liberty of future generations, we must educate the current generations about the value of free speech, not just about its perceived "downside." People who believe in free speech and uninhibited debate on campus must stop feeling that they need to qualify or apologize for those essential beliefs. The messy, loud, chaotic and, yes, sometimes-offensive nature of a college campus is what makes the college experience compelling and unique. College administrators' time would be far better spent preparing students for how to dive in and take full advantage of this chaotic paradise, rather than trying to corral all the most vocal students into tiny free-speech zones.

Besides, as my math whiz friend has warned me, if we have to pack students any more tightly together than at Texas Tech, we may end up with a black hole on our hands, and nobody wants that.

7

Hate Speech Is Unfitting in a Democracy

Zack Beauchamp

Zack Beauchamp serves as world correspondent at Vox.com and writes about public policy. He previously served as a political editor at ThinkProgress and contributed to The Dish. He has also worked with Newsweek and The Daily Beast. Beauchamp attended the London School of Economics and Political Science.

When then-candidate Donald Trump seemed to fan the flames of fear and discord amongst his supporters during the 2016 presidential campaign, millions of Americans were enraged — and that rage inspired the author of this article to express his own anger. Though he falls short of equating Trump's words with hate speech, he believes they emboldened groups that espouse hate. The prediction of election-day violence never materialized, but Beauchamp proves prophetic in regard to the push for legitimacy among previously dormant right-wing hate groups.

Donald Trump's claim that the upcoming election is rigged against him is without precedent in modern US history. The potential consequences are bigger than you think.

The GOP candidate's talk of "millions" of fraudulent votes and his commitment to only accept the election results "if I win" don't sound like the words of a typical American politician, and

"Make America Violent Again: Trump's Rhetoric Could Cause Election Day Mayhem— and Worse," by Zack Beauchamp, Vox Media, October 26, 2016. Reprinted by permission.

for good reason: The typical American politician has faith in the system, accepts the results of an election, and moves on.

Trump is doing something very different, pairing rhetoric about a rigged election with a message that basically says it's him or the apocalypse. He has repeatedly warned his fans that if he loses, the America they know will be irreparably damaged.

Those kinds of words can have serious real-world impact. A range of scholars who study everything from civil wars to the history of the Ku Klux Klan each expressed deep concern about potential consequences ranging from murders at polling booths to the rise of a new racist terrorist movement to the weakening of the long-term stability of the American political system.

It's important to emphasize that none of these outcomes is especially likely. If Trump loses, as now seems quite likely, things will probably be fine: Mass violence can only erupt under a specific set of circumstances, and American democracy has withstood an actual civil war, not to mentions decades of racially motivated unrest. Many right-wingers are also known for talking a big game but then ultimately backing down without a fight.

But it's the "probably" that keeps me up at night. Trump is making some pretty catastrophic events more likely than they should be. And that should really scare us.

"It really is hard to think of democratic politicians who've done this — anywhere," says Shaun Bowler, a professor of political science at the University of California Riverside who studies the behavior of parties that lose at the ballot box. "He's done quite a bit of damage already."

It's not just a campaign about who will be the president anymore. It's a campaign about what kind of country America will be after the votes are cast.

There Is a Serious Risk of Violence on Election Day, and it Is Trump's Fault

The first major test of Trump's inflammatory language about a stolen election will come on Election Day itself. Trump has been encouraging his supporters, who are heavily white and non-urban, to "go around and watch other polling places." He has specifically told his supporters to watch polling places in urban areas; the racial subtext isn't exactly subtle.

"I hear these horror shows, and we have to make sure that this election is not stolen from us and is not taken away from us," he said at one rally in Pennsylvania. "And everybody knows what I'm talking about."

Basically, Trump is encouraging his voters, already anxious about a possibly "rigged" election, to go out to polling places full of non-Trump voters and serve as amateur election police. These people can't go into polling places, legally speaking. But they can congregate around polling places, showing up and harassing voters waiting in line.

It's a situation you can easily imagine escalating out of control.

A fight breaks out between a Trump supporter and, say, a Black Lives Matter advocate — and one of them is armed. A radical Trump supporter, perhaps a member of a far-right militia or neo-Nazi movement, shows up at a polling station with the intent of using force to stop minorities from "rigging" the vote. It could also go the other way: A Hispanic American or African American tired of being demonized by Trump could see one of his supporters and go looking for a fight.

Trump "claims that the stakes are so high, the situation is so extraordinary, that some form of intimidation, presence, provocative behavior is necessary to preserve the republic, preserve civilization," says Paul Staniland, a University of Chicago professor who studies violence and civil conflict. "This kind of rhetoric raises the probability [of electoral violence]. I'm comfortable drawing a straight line."

Indeed, some of Trump's supporters — especially from the loose-knit network of far-right political groups and militias -- are now openly talking about post-election bloodshed. According to a January count by the Southern Poverty Law Center, there are 276 such militias operating in the United States. A review of 240 militia group Facebook pages by researcher Jonathon Morgan found a spike in their online activity in recent months — with some members openly warning of the need for violence if Clinton wins.

"If she wins ... it's over, time for a revolution," one militia member writes, according to Morgan. "Enough of being tough on the blogs, be tough in real life."

Trump and his aides consistently and angrily deny using irresponsible language that raises the risk of civil unrest. The problem is that violence could erupt all the same because of the atmosphere of paranoia that Trump has helped create.

Trump's rhetoric surround his plan to ban Muslim immigration, which often implies all Muslims are potential terrorists, is a case in point. A new report from the Center for the Study of Hate and Extremism at California State University San Bernardino found that 2015 saw the highest rate of anti-Muslim hate crimes since the period directly after 9/11.

Some of that is doubtless due to the hundreds killed by ISIS terrorists around the globe, including the 49 people massacred at a gay nightclub in Orlando in the worst terror attack in the US in more than 15 years. But experts say Trump is leading many of his supporters to use those attacks to conflate ISIS with Islam and treat ordinary Muslim Americans as potential threats.

"You have politicians talking about deporting Muslims and saying that the vetting process isn't good enough," Daryl Johnson, a former Department of Homeland Security analyst and expert on right-wing violence, told the Kansas City Star. "So people start thinking that ISIS is around every corner."

There's an X factor in the United States that makes the situation particularly scary: guns.

The United States has the highest rate of gun ownership in the world, by far. I don't mean in the developed world: The country with the next closest level of gun ownership is Yemen, which has a little over half as many guns per person as the United States.

Laws in many states allow people to carry their guns with them, either concealed or openly, even during political demonstrations. Many gun owners explicitly see their firearms as checks on potential government tyranny.

There's just no analogous situation to this, especially where a leading politician is explicitly encouraging his followers to see the electoral system as corrupt and broken.

"You have preexisting, organized, armed militias who have said that they might see it as their duty ... to attempt violently to topple the government or kill the president," Jay Ulfelder, a political scientist who studies democracy and violence, says. "I can't think of any other case where there's been something like that, either in a developed democracy or less [developed one]."

The prevalence of gun ownership makes Trump's rhetoric far riskier. In one scenario, as Ulfelder suggests, you have right-wing radicals actively believing that Trump is encouraging them to take up arms against their own government. In another, the presence of guns could cause a fight between two citizens to turn from punches to bullets.

In the truly scary scenario, one or several such incidents get amplified, inspiring other acts of violence either on Election Day or directly afterward. Then you get a wave of violence around the country.

"This is what I worry about with social media and the media in general," Staniland frets. "This could escalate very quickly across a wide variety of localized areas. I think that's the big danger about short-term violence linked to this campaign."

If bloodshed erupts on Election Day, it will be a dark echo of an earlier and much more tumultuous period of American history. Most Americans have forgotten how rough our elections used to be. But early in the republic, political violence was the norm, not the exception. "Until 1896, not a single Election Day passed in the United States without someone getting killed at the polls," historian Jill Lepore writes in the New Yorker.

The most notable period of election-related violence came during Reconstruction, the Northern effort to rebuild the South after the Civil War and empower black citizens. The postwar attempt by black leaders to organize for elections and political participation directly led to the rise of groups like the Ku Klux Klan.

The Klan itself was founded in Pulaski, Tennessee — a town that was, at the time, notable for having a relatively wealthy and politically connected black population. Initially, the Klan wasn't especially violent, serving as more of a social club for former Confederate soldiers. But as time went on and the white population grew more concerned about black social power, the Klan took matters into its own hands.

By the 1868 presidential election, the Klan was regularly intimidating Pulaski's prominent black residents, showing up at their homes and threatening them with harm if they asserted themselves politically. The goal of this violent turn was to destroy Pulaski's black civil society, to make sure that black people wouldn't be able to get to the polls in great numbers or hold political office.

"It becomes clear to [whites] that they're not going to be allowed to rebuild their own power structure," says Elaine Parsons, a historian at Duquesne University and the author of Ku-Klux: The Birth of the Klan during Reconstruction. "They can see black groups mobilizing, and so they're concerned that they're building up a civic infrastructure."

This intimidation wave evolved into the South-wide campaign of terrorist violence and murder, most notably lynchings, the group is remembered for.

According to Parsons, the spread of the Klan wasn't centrally organized by some headquarters in Pulaski. Instead, its branches across the nation were mostly independent, starting up in their town or region basically without direction.

The key factor in its spread? Outsize media coverage of Klan violence, which inspired like-minded whites around the country to take up arms under the Klan banner. Media coverage of one violent attack on black political organizing generated more such attacks.

"Disparate groups organized themselves in response to learning about the Klan in the media," Parsons says. "It was a pretty organic expression of white fear about black power."

Trump Isn't Just Stoking Electoral Violence — He's Undermining Confidence in Elections Themselves

Those are precisely the types of fears that Trump is trying to capitalize on today, pairing "rigged election" rhetoric with terrifying warnings about the end of America. He has repeatedly told his fans that if he loses, they might not get another chance at a fair election.

"I think this will be the last election if I don't win," Trump said in a September appearance on the Christian Broadcasting Network. "You're going to have illegal immigrants coming in and they're going to be legalized and they're going to be able to vote, and once that all happens, you can forget it."

Trump is arguing that his defeat would be proof that the system is rigged against him and its outcome fraudulent and illegitimate. That, the University of Chicago's Staniland says, "undermines faith in the democratic system, that the votes will be counted in a free and fair way."

You can already see the impact of Trump's incessant fearmongering. A September Gallup poll found that only half of Republicans were confident that their votes would be counted accurately, the lowest number ever in a Gallup poll on this issue. A late October poll, from Reuters, found that 70 percent of Trump supporters believe a Clinton victory would be a result of "illegal voting or vote rigging." Only 50 percent of Trump backers, in this poll, say they'd accept Clinton as their president.

There's every reason to expect this to get worse in the next two weeks — and even after the election.

Prior to Barack Obama's election, data showed Republicans having slightly more confidence in the fairness of US election than Democrats. But in surveys conducted during and after the 2008 and 2012 elections, this flipped. Republicans started to believe in widespread voter fraud, like people pretending to be someone else at the ballot box, at higher rates than Democrats.

This can partly be attributed to the elections' results. A significant number of studies, both in the United States and internationally, show that people's confidence in the electoral system is determined by whether their candidate has won. So when George W. Bush was elected president, Republicans had more faith in the system; once Obama won, Democrats did.

Republicans have also spent much of the past decade pushing laws requiring voters to show IDs before they can vote, arguing that the US voting system is racked with fraud and requires a legislative change to fix it. Democrats, by contrast, have argued that such changes actually undermine electoral fairness by disenfranchising a lot of poor and minority voters, who tend to have fewer government-issued IDs and a harder time obtaining them.

The result is that the issues of voter fraud and election legitimacy have become highly politicized, with many Republican voters believing that voting fraud is widespread.

These two trends, taken together, are very worrying for this election. First, they tell us that losing undermines voters' faith in the system. Second, they tell us that many Republican are already predisposed to believe the electoral system is rigged.

Trump is losing — and he's saying it's because the system is rigged. His hardcore supporters, who see the electoral system through the lens of how Trump does and what Trump he them about that result, will almost certainly take his rhetoric seriously.

This is why experts on fairness in elections, like Harvard political scientist Pippa Norris and UC Riverside's Bowler, are so worried about Trump's rhetoric. They understand that faith in the legitimacy of the electoral system is more fragile than Americans generally believe — so when a major party nominee takes a hammer to it, the candidate can undermine the system far more than you might otherwise think.

Election Day Could Be Bad. What Comes Next Could Be Worse

No matter how heated the rhetoric, both sides have historically accepted the outcomes of US elections even when they had reason to question their legitimacy. Consider the 2000 presidential election: Democrats had a lot of good reasons to think the White House was, in a way, stolen from Al Gore. Yet Gore conceded after the Supreme Court ruled in Bush's favor, and Democrats mostly reconciled themselves to a Bush administration.

What Trump has done is radically different, and the impact of his rhetoric will live on long after November 8, even if that's all it ends up being in the end — rhetoric.

"There will be a proportion of the American public that views this election as fundamentally illegitimate, even if Trump concedes," Staniland says. "He's sowed the seeds of radical doubt, in ways that will be difficult to reel back in even if he wanted to — and I don't think he particularly wants to."

Indeed, there's good evidence that Trump will just keep on Trumping after his likely defeat. His campaign has begun airing a nightly news show on its Facebook page, which is widely understood to be a test run for launching an entire Trump TV station or a digital-only, subscription-based media operation modeled on Glenn Beck's troubled site The Blaze. Trump's son-in-law Jared Kushner has already reached out to an influential TV investor; his campaign CEO, Steve Bannon, has played coy when asked about a potential venture, telling reporters that "Trump is an entrepreneur."

Trump TV would likely continue and amplify the kind of racialized, conspiratorial rhetoric you've seen from his campaign — clearly, it's been a key part of his brand. He would provide a much bigger platform for the fringe right, figures like the conspiracy theorist Alex Jones, than it had before. The network would hammer home the message that the system itself is illegitimate and American democracy is being stolen, beaming it to every hardcore Trump fan with an internet connection.

The potential for long-term damage, from both Trump's campaign rhetoric and a Trump TV network, are severe. And that's because they intersect terribly with America's most fundamental political divide: race.

Trump's base, according to the best political science evidence we have, is overwhelmingly driven by racial resentment. As the United States has become more ethnically diverse, a portion of white Americans have become increasingly anxious about the future of their country. They feel a sense of loss, of alienation from a society that doesn't look like the one they grew up in. The result is their support for the most nakedly racist demagogue since George Wallace.

In developing countries, this kind of ethnic power transfer is the exact situation where widespread ethnic conflict breaks out.

A 2010 paper published in the journal World Politics looked at 157 cases of ethnic violence in nations ranging from Chad to Lebanon. It found strong statistical correlations between one group's decline in status and the likelihood that the group turns to violence against another group. This suggests that eight years of governance by a black president would inflame white racial panic, a sentiment borne out by the data on white attitudes during the Obama years.

According to Erica Chenoweth, a political scientist at the University of Denver, this violence becomes particularly likely when members of the former majority no longer trust political institutions to function fairly. Institutions like, say, elections.

The scenario that kept coming up in my interviews is a resurgence of anti-government, racially motivated terrorism.

In this case, whites inspired by Trump's rigged election rhetoric form militant groups, or join existing militias, as a way of retaking their country from Clinton's heavily minority coalition. If they believe the system no longer treats them fairly, they might decide to attack it.

"If Hillary wins, I think you will see civil violence [targeting] the government," Chenoweth says. "That's my political science prediction."

Parsons, for her part, sees a lot of similarities between what's happening right now and the sort of backlash that fueled the KKK's popularity during Reconstruction.

"It's very scary; I find this very familiar," she says. "My suspicion is that the Klan, and Klan groups, will in fact be coming back in a fairly substantial way. ... The Klan is the tip of the iceberg of an anti-black anxiety that Trump is fueling."

It's import to recognize that the vast, vast majority of Trump supporters — even those with racist or anti-immigrant views — are unlikely to turn to violence in any form. But it doesn't take many people to mount a sustained campaign of anti-government or anti-minority violence. It just takes a few determined people, and communities that are alienated enough from the system to shelter them. Think of the Oklahoma City bombing, for example.

"You don't need that many people to basically start a major national crisis," as Chenoweth puts it.

Of course, this is just one possible outcome. Predicting the long-term effects of something like Trump's rhetoric is extremely difficult. Statistics aren't wizardry, and political scientists don't have crystal balls.

The point, more fundamentally, is that mucking with the democratic system itself is extremely dangerous. Democracies are not invulnerable, especially ones that have been riven by ethnic divides for literally their entire existence. The effects of undermining faith in the system, the thing most responsible for keeping the peace, are in many ways totally unpredictable.

"There's potential, between a variety of social movements and a lot of armed citizens, for really some pretty surprisingly unstable dynamics to emerge," Staniland says. "It's not that far in the history books."

Will this lead to some kind of major crisis, created by right-wing terrorism or some other social unrest, that threatens to sunder American democracy? Like any long-term prediction, it's difficult to say with confidence — and I don't want to be alarmist, issuing Cassandra-like warnings of a crisis that's fairly unlikely to happen.

But the fact that we're even talking about this, and political scientists and historians are taking it seriously rather than laughing it off, is quite telling.

"After the wave of democratization 20 years ago, what you got was all kinds of people from Ukraine, Argentina, Mexico — all of those places that didn't have strong institutions — looking to the US for examples," says Bowler. "We're talking to people now who are experts on Ukraine, or Mexico, for lessons about what's going to happen in the US. That, in itself, is a very worrisome fact."

Trump is attacking the core democratic institutions that it has taken Americans years to build up, raising issues about electoral legitimacy and trust in the system that are basically unheard of in longstanding, wealthy democracies. Clinton is likely to win the election. But American democracy might end up losing all the same.

8

What If Hate Speech Were Criminalized?

Hadewina Snijders and Ruth Shoemaker Wood

Hadewina Snijders and Ruth Shoemaker Wood are senior fellows for Humanity in Action an international educational organization seeks to educate, inspire, and connect a global network of students, as well as young professionals and established leaders. The non-profit organization works to promote human rights, diversity and active citizenship within individual communities.

The authors of this article delve into the precedences in limiting hate speech in order to gain knowledge about its drawbacks and benefits. They cite such a law in the Netherlands and conclude that it is ideal, despite gray area, to embrace a system with unfettered freedom of speech no matter how odious the message, though they concede the advantages of such limits. The authors studied wide-ranging views to give credence to their opinions, including those of two Holocaust survivors and one extreme-right activist.

In approaching the topic of the criminalization of hate speech in the Netherlands, it was necessary as an American-Dutch team to bring our own culturally-indoctrinated ideas about freedom of speech to the drawing board at the outset of our working relationship. A few weeks ago our outlooks on limiting speech were significantly different than we find them to be after having explored in depth this complicated issue. From an American

"The Criminalization of Hate Speech in the Netherlands," by Hadewina Snijders and Ruth Shoemaker Wood, Humanity in Action. Reprinted by permission.

standpoint, the idea of limiting free speech sounded foreign, oppressive, and against the aims of any first-world democracy that claimed to promote human rights. From a Dutch perspective, the idea of not placing limitations on speech sounded like a sure-fire way to promote violence, terrorism, and complete disregard for human rights.

Over the course of interviewing a professor, a journalist, two Holocaust survivors, and an extreme-right activist and engaging in detailed discussion and reading on the topic, we observed gradual transformations and complications arise out of our formerly held and, for the most part, unquestioned beliefs. In this paper we aim to present objectively the various views and complexities that came out of our interviews and to present these views in conversation with each other. With regard to some of the issues we address, we have come to clear-cut conclusions about how we each personally feel. With regard to other issues, however, we have gained a deeper understanding of the complexities involved, yet continue to struggle personally with nuanced, philosophical underpinnings. Our attempt in this paper was not to arrive at one neatly packaged conclusion, but rather to gain a deeper appreciation for multiple culturally-influenced ways of looking at the criminalization of hate speech in the Netherlands and to begin to clarify in our own minds our personal stances on a multi-faceted challenge facing present-day society.

International Human Rights Law and the Netherlands

The complex structure of international human rights law since 1945 has been constructed as a moral answer to the Nazi ideology of racism. The primary focus of human rights since 1945 has been efforts to guarantee freedom from discrimination on grounds of race, gender, or religious belief. The 1948 Human Rights Convention of Geneva spoke directly to Holocaust atrocities of World War II. Two decades later, over 125 countries have ratified the main international treaty against racial discrimination, the

International Convention on the Elimination of All Forms of Racial Discrimination (CERD) of 1966. Other treaties aiming to ensure freedom from discrimination include Article 19 of the Universal Declaration of Human Rights (UDHR), the International Covenant on Civil and Political Rights (ICCPR), and the Convention for the Protection of Human Rights and Fundamental Freedoms. Although Article 1 of the Dutch Constitution prohibits discrimination, courts may not rule legislation unconstitutional, but may instead invoke certain provisions of the international anti-discrimination treaties mentioned above. Because the Netherlands lacks its own comprehensive anti-discrimination act, it often occurs that the above-mentioned anti-discrimination provisions are referred to in the court system (Coliver 1-7).

Complicating freedom from discrimination is the issue of ensuring freedom of speech in a society. A clear divide exists between the approach toward freedom of speech advocated by the United States and that advocated by the Netherlands. In the US, the balance is struck in favor of freedom of speech without limitation, whereas in the Netherlands, the balance is struck in favor of the belief that racist speech must be limited under conditions prescribed by law (Coliver 1-7).

Out of the Dutch ratification of the CERD in 1971 came an expansion of Dutch criminal law towards limiting the public expression of hate speech. Because of increasing hate speech in the late 1980s and early 1990s and new waves of anti-Semitism throughout Europe, the Dutch government committed itself to enforcing stricter limitations on racist speech and criminalized Holocaust denial. 1994, for example, marked the first time in Dutch history that political party leaders were personally convicted based on their official party platform when leaders of the Centrumdemocraten party were prosecuted for the espousal of their extreme-right ideology. Additionally, the political party itself was convicted the same year for its racist agenda. Also rooted in a more direct commitment on the part of the Dutch government to limiting and prosecuting hate speech is the difficulty extreme-right groups face when attempting to secure permits for public events and demonstrations (van Donselaar 32).

Ideological vs. Pragmatic Approaches

In analyzing the opposing perspectives of various individuals involved directly as professors and reporters in the ongoing dialogue surrounding hate speech as well as those involved indirectly as citizens living under the limitations imposed by the Dutch government, it is essential to distinguish between what Dr. Jaap van Donselaar, of the Anne Frank Foundation and Leiden University, explains as the principle or ideological view of the debate on one hand and the pragmatic view on the other hand. "There exist so many different views on this topic because people approach it from two distinct levels," he explains. He reveals that many of the discussions in which he has participated tend to become quite confusing as participants mix up these distinct approaches. The ideological way of conceptualizing the debate on criminalizing hate speech is "a way of thinking about democracy and political rights" based on fundamental principles that disregard actual implementation. The pragmatic way of addressing the situation does not concern itself with philosophical principles, but rather examines the probable tangible societal effects of maintaining or curbing limitations on free speech.

Just as Van Donselaar has observed the difficulties that arise when those with opposing viewpoints attempt to reach mutual understanding by way of opposing approaches, we observe throughout our discussion that follows the nuanced complications that arise when reporters, journalists, politicians, and citizens approach the topic from either an ideological or pragmatic perspective. An additional complication interestingly arises when individuals subtly switch from one approach to the other throughout the course of their argument.

Inherent Contradiction of Basic Human Rights

A recurring theme that surfaced in discussions about the criminalization of hate speech centered around the idea that basic human rights are, by definition, often at odds with each other and, as a result, present complex challenges when one attempts to forego or limit one right in favor of preserving the purity of another. At the crux of our exploration of limiting hate speech in the Netherlands is the multi-faceted challenge of simultaneously protecting the right of individuals to express opposing opinions and the right of individuals not to be the objects of discrimination. Both the right to freedom from discrimination and the right to freedom of expression are protected in the Dutch Constitution in Articles 1 and 7 respectively and these rights are viewed as holding equal importance (Boerefijn 206). Implicit in this lack of hierarchy is the question of what occurs when a situation arises that calls into question both freedoms. As Boerefijn explains: In cases where... rights are found to be in conflict, they are weighed against each other within the framework of Parliament's constitutional authority to impose limitations on them...The government believes that this constitutional system guarantees a carefully balanced relationship between the exercise of one right and respect for another (206).

Not all observers of this system are satisfied, however. Rinke van den Brink, a reporter at the weekly publication Vrij Nederland who has been covering the extreme right since 1983, understands the complexities involved in finding a solution that allows freedom of speech without risking discrimination, but he explains, "I'm rather afraid of solving problems by forbidding [freedom of speech]. It [discrimination] will not disappear because it cannot be said aloud." Dr. van Donselaar agrees that, by definition, basic human rights are often at odds with each other. Consequently, he believes that "it's not a matter of limiting or not limiting [certain rights]; it's a matter of when and under what circumstances [to do so in order] to limit violence, terrorism..."

Van den Brink's commitment to the importance of ensuring free speech can be analyzed as stemming from an ideological commitment based on a highly principled view of the role that freedom of expression plays in a society, whereas Van Donselaar's argument is based on a more pragmatic attempt to foresee and address the tangible effects that unlimited speech might have on individuals in a society. Thus, the question remains of how to strike a livable balance between freedom of speech and freedom from discrimination. This discussion increases in complexity as experts like Van den Brink and Van Donselaar approach it from ideological or pragmatic levels that are challenging to reconcile.

Hate Speech and Human Nature

While one hope is that limiting what people can say will, over time, lead to a decrease in racism by changing the way they think, Holocaust survivor Frieda Menco emphasizes her belief that it is human nature to hate and discriminate against others. She believes that hate speech is prevalent in society for this reason and she explains that if minorities were not the targets of racist sentiment in modern-day Germany, for example, "it might be bad for the Jews again...People seem to need groups to despise because in despising someone else, you see yourself as wonderful...I think we all have to check ourselves for that constantly. We all have that inclination in us." She continues by explaining that cultural differences lie at the core of discrimination: "The unknown, the difference of culture, causes a lot of discrimination. The only thing that helps is getting to know people and getting to know that they have the same heart and soul and liver."

Self-described National Socialist agitator and vocal member of the extreme-right, Joop Glimmerveen has been imprisoned three times for the expression of his extreme political beliefs and presently faces another three-month sentence for a hate speech incident three years ago. He agrees that it is in the nature of human beings to discriminate and also believes that discrimination is rooted in difference and feelings of superiority. While he says that he is "infamous for hate speech and discrimination" he rejects the suggestion that his party, the Dutch People's Union

(Nederlandse Volks Unie), engages in hate speech. "We agitate against foreigners. That is not hate speech. We are doing nothing to them. We only don't want them in the Netherlands," he explains. Glimmerveen does not consider his message hate speech, but rather "a political statement" motivated by "political beliefs and idealism." Glimmerveen has been disseminating his "idealism" in the Netherlands as chairman of the extreme-right Dutch People's Union from 1974 until 1986 and again from 1996 until early-June 2000 when an organizational power struggle caused him to step down from the position.

The Extreme-Right's Seduction of the Defenseless

Ms. Menco approaches the discussion on limiting freedom of speech in the Netherlands from a distinctly pragmatic viewpoint as she explains her fear of extreme-right groups, if given unlimited opportunity to espouse their racist messages, appealing to juveniles and to those without the capacity to understand the implications of their messages. "Not the whole world consists of bright people so they listen to hate speech because of course it's a way of being nice to yourself," she explains, echoing her belief that discrimination occurs because in presenting others in a negative light, people feel more positive about themselves. Ms. Menco supports limitations on freedom of expression and is acutely aware of the danger the extreme-right presents to those she considers defenseless: "When you have a group together [i.e. an extreme-right group] and when you attract young people, you are dangerous...I think a lot of people are, in fact, defenseless because they are not able to think critically." Holocaust survivor Berry Dotsch shares Ms. Menco's fears that extreme-right groups depend on membership from young people and those who are defenseless.

Journalist Rinke van den Brink understands but finds fault with Ms. Menco's fears about the extreme right appealing to young people and to people of lower intelligence: "Frankly spoken, she might be right. I understand what she means, of course. But I think it's a very elitist view...There's only one way to protect people from being seduced by undemocratic parties--to ameliorate their lives, to get them jobs, houses..." Van den Brink explains that it is the task of the school system to prepare students to be responsible, critically-thinking citizens who will not be easy targets of extreme-right groups.

When questioned about the ease that Menco believes his group has in seducing juveniles and the defenseless, Glimmerveen emphasizes that "we don't look for them; they come to us." Nonetheless, he reveals that his party is "rapidly growing" and almost one hundred percent of the growth can be attributed to people between the ages of fifteen and thirty-two. He boasts that his is the youngest party in the Netherlands, based on average age of members.

Just as Van den Brink espouses a view of schools playing a fundamental role in the education of independent thinkers and responsible citizens, Glimmerveen harshly criticizes schools for limiting political views by promoting only one liberal perspective and, in doing so, acting against the aims of public education. He specifically rails against the educational system for influencing youth to hold views in favor of the multi-racial society and for failing to present the right-wing point of view which he holds: that immigrants and asylum seekers should be removed from the Netherlands "for the integrity of our people. The multi-racial society is a failure; it's a despair, a catastrophe."

Limitations and the Changing Nature of the Extreme-Right

Glimmerveen's explanation that the Dutch People's Union is "rapidly growing" calls into question the hopes of many that criminalizing hate speech in the Netherlands will lead to a decrease in the size of extreme right groups and a change in their mentality toward a less overtly racist stance. Despite reports such as Glimmerveen's that extreme-right groups are increasing in size even with limitations in place, Dr. van Donselaar supports limitations aimed at curbing hate speech and believes in their effectiveness. In attempting to reconcile his ideological and pragmatic approaches to the debate, he explains: "Principally spoken, I'm not in favor of limiting freedom of speech. On a more practical level, I have observed in the international research that it really works against organized racism." Here, Van Donselaar reveals that he perceives limitations as working specifically against extreme-right groups more directly than against individuals. Berry Dotsch echoes Van Donselaar's sentiments that limitations on hate speech are necessary in counteracting organized racism: "If freedom of speech was not limited," he explains, "the danger is that [the extreme-right] would grow in size because there is always room for fascism."

Thus, critics like Dotsch and Van Donselaar support limitations on free speech as an obstacle used to deter racist ideas from being disseminated in society. Van Donselaar finds the act of "placing more doors and more gates and more barriers and more hurdles" in the way of the extreme-right an effective mechanism that decreases their activities. He emphasizes, however, that criminalizing hate speech is just one obstacle that can be utilized to deter racist expression. He also notes the roles that negative media attention and the risk of stigmatization play in decreasing the strength of the extreme-right by decreasing the inclination of potential members to join. He discusses the risk faced by post-war extreme-right leaders of being labeled a Neo-Nazi, an anti-Semite, or a political criminal and explains that potential members of extreme-right parties are less inclined to associate themselves with a group that holds these labels and runs the risk of being prosecuted or banned. As a result, Van Donselaar explains, gaining mass support under these conditions is difficult and extreme-right organizations, contrary to what Glimmerveen reports, do not gain in popular support. Van Donselaar emphasizes that limiting the expression that is tolerated from the extreme-right does not attempt to change the way they think and to make members less racist through education. Rather: it's an approach through threat, the threat of being prosecuted, the threat of being banned. It doesn't affect the mentality of hard-core extremists, but it does influence the way of thinking of those who don't want to be part of a criminal group or associated with a group linked with second world war fascism. Additionally, Van Donselaar cites the negative media attention which the extreme-right attracts. This non-neutral coverage influences people's decisions not to join the extreme-right as well.

Criminalizing hate speech also succeeds in decreasing the potency of the extreme-right, according to Van Donselaar, by forcing groups to become more moderate. When pressured to restrain their racist expression, extreme-right groups refine their message to one that includes less overt racism. In moving toward this more moderate positioning, they risk little distinction between group political profiles which leads to potential members opting to join other groups that are not associated with the stigmas that extreme-right groups have collected. As gaining member support becomes more difficult, fissions within groups lead to organizational instability among the extreme-right. Interestingly, Glimmerveen reiterates Van Donselaar's belief that criminalizing hate speech changes the nature of political parties, but he suggests not that the extreme-right becomes more moderate, but rather that other groups that subtly espouse rightest agendas mask these agendas behind facades of liberalism and, in doing so, gain more mass support than extreme-right groups that espouse similar philosophies in a more open manner. As support for this position, Glimmerveen claims that the Volkspartij voor Vrijheid en Democratie (VVD), a liberal party in the Netherlands, holds the same anti-immigrant ideas that the extreme-right Dutch People's Union espouses, yet the VVD gains more support because in presenting their ideas more covertly, they avoid the stigmas associated with the extreme-right.

Limitations and Racist Mentality

While the nature of extreme-right political parties is, perhaps, affected by limitations on free speech, it remains unclear whether decreasing the amount of hate speech tolerated in a society actually leads to decreased levels of racist thought and action. Changing mentality, however, is not the aim, Van Donselaar clarifies in his comment that limiting hate speech is "not an educational approach toward changing mentality," but rather an attempt, as outlined above, to put obstructions in the path of the extreme-right in an attempt to limit through threat and stigmatization the dissemination of their views. In keeping with his belief that changing racist mentality is not the primary aim of hate speech limitations, he explains that "just because people's opinions aren't being changed by laws doesn't mean we should throw away the penal code and not prosecute crimes."

Extreme Right Party Politics and Free Speech

Our research suggests that the present limitations on freedom of speech in place in the Netherlands are aimed more directly at the extreme right than at individuals espousing racist views. With this distinction in mind, it is essential to examine opposing viewpoints on how limitations on freedom of speech apply and should apply to political parties as organizations in the Netherlands. Two very distinct and, to some degree, irreconcilable philosophies arise from this debate: one side focuses on the need, outlined above, to obstruct extreme-right parties with the aim in mind to decrease their potency; the other side holds as its mantra that "in a free society tolerance requires us to tolerate the intolerable" (Tuerk and Joinet 50). Van den Brink opposes limitations on free speech, regardless of whether those limitations are aimed at extreme right parties or individuals. He is committed to upholding rights to free speech for the extreme-right, calling this stance "a very ugly position to defend," but emphasizing that "people have the right to their opinions." Here, he unquestioningly links attempts to limit free speech with attempts to limit free thought and this idea is one he finds extremely problematic. In discussing the role that extreme right parties play in the Netherlands today, he introduces the challenge of dealing with "people who use democracy to someday abolish it." With regard to this struggle, he emphasizes that "you must be very careful about using undemocratic methods against organizations with undemocratic aims, even if they play the game by the rules of democracy."

While Van den Brink strongly opposes limiting the expressions of the extreme right, he concedes that the law must be used occasionally to remind these groups that they are being closely monitored: You cannot forbid people to have ideas, even stupid or racist ideas, so I don't believe in the effectiveness of repression. But, on the other hand, if you have laws, you can't allow people to constantly break these laws, so I do support prosecuting from time to time people who go too far, who put the deed with the word. In a way, it's to let them know that they are watched, that they can't do something without consequences. Here, Van den Brink reveals that he supports occasional prosecution, but he makes it clear that prosecution should only result when a racist act has actually been committed that stems from racist expression. He does not support prosecution for expression alone. Because of the complications inherent in this distinction, Van den Brink believes that pragmatically, political parties should not be forbidden until after they cross the line of putting "the deed with the word." He also opposes forbidding a political party for acts committed by a few members, even if these members are leaders, and equates this action with "shooting a tiny fly with a big gun."

Van den Brink vocally opposes Van Donselaar's interest in using limitations on free speech and various other measures to obstruct extreme right parties. He cites Mr. Hans Janmaat's extreme-right Centrumdemocraten party that gained a seat in Parliament in 1994 on a platform advocating the end of multicultural society in the Netherlands. "No one protested against this program during elections," Van den Brink stated. "Two years after his election, Janmaat addressed the first public rally his party had ever held and quoted his electoral platform, telling the 'crowd:' if we get the power, we end multicultural society. Although the platform of the Centrumdemocraten had never been subject to any charges, the public prosecutor now charged Janmaat with racial hatred and discrimination." In response to this case, Van den Brink explains that "in a parliamentary democracy, I think that when a party is accepted in elections...you gave this party an approval which you cannot easily withdraw [by way of attempts to obstruct and limit the party's political message]." He continues by explaining that if a party has succeeded in gaining the votes needed for a seat in Parliament, it has a right to a place to meet and a right to express its views without limitation. Once a part of Parliament, it is undemocratic, from Van den Brink's perspective, to place limitations on a political party. With regard to prosecuting hate speech, Ms. Menco and Mr. Dotsch present a viewpoint in opposition to that of Van den Brink: that insulting, offensive expression must be prosecuted. "I think especially when you are a person who has not been protected in life...it gives you a good feeling when you are living in a country where hate speech is forbidden by law," Ms. Menco explains. She continues that if she were living in a country without limitations on hate speech, she would feel much more threatened because of her background. "The law is made to protect us," adds Mr. Dotsch, referring to targets of hate speech including Jews and ethnic minorities.

While Dotsch sees the goal of the law as protecting minorities, Glimmerveen has a very different perspective: "Anti-discrimination laws are used to put down politicians who are a danger for the establishment. They always say that a strong democracy must not be scared, but they are scared." Glimmerveen echoes the beliefs expressed by Van den Brink that a free society demands the right to free speech for all political parties. In support of this view is the outlook reported by Tuerk and Joinet: "Democracy is indeed a 'tragic' political system, for it is the only regime that openly faces the possibility of its self-destruction by taking up the challenge of offering its enemies the means of contesting it (38)." From Glimmerveen's perspective, it is this view that lies at the heart of the fear he points to that motivates those around him to attempt to limit the expression of his rightest agenda. Glimmerveen points out that "when you don't have freedom of speech for a political party, you can't change something fundamental." While Glimmerveen vehemently opposes limiting the speech of political parties in the Netherlands, he concedes that it is acceptable for hate speech "on a personal level" to be punished. He defines personally-directed hate speech as racially or ethnically insulting attacks made by groups or individuals against other individuals in a setting outside the realm of politics. At the same time, however, he strictly and vocally opposes inter-racial marriage which can certainly be viewed as falling outside the realm of the political and inside the realm of the personal.

The Risk of Driving the Extreme-Right Underground

Arising from and complicating the debate surrounding criminalizing hate speech is the fear of some that enforcing limitations will drive racist expression underground where it is more difficult to monitor. From his background as a journalist, Van den Brink explains that it is easier to "put informants in or to find informers within, a party with, say, 400 members, than in 20 groups with 15 to 20 members that know each other far better." While Dotsch remains loyal to his belief that prosecuting must occur when groups or individuals participate in insulting or offensive speech, he struggles with reconciling his ideological and pragmatic view on limitations. He explains that ideologically he would opt for forbidding extreme-right expression, but concedes that perhaps it is more practical not to completely forbid because "it will drive them underground where it's more difficult to watch them." He reconciles these views by supporting limitations on speech, but opposing complete banning of extreme-right parties.

Conclusion

After examining various sides of the issue of the criminalization of hate speech in the Netherlands through the eyes of a professor, a reporter, two Holocaust survivors, and an extreme-right activist, we observed that, to some extent, we refined our deeply-held, culturally-instilled beliefs about the role that freedom of speech plays in democratic society. We recognize that there exist many compelling reasons why limitations on free speech enhance the democratic nature of society and we clearly understand how a perceived need for limitations imposed on hate speech would exist in post-Holocaust Europe. Nevertheless, even with the trade-offs and benefits that must be foregone in order to protect complete freedom of speech, we are personally committed to a system in which citizens can, without limitation, voice their beliefs and opinions, regardless of how reprehensible these positions may be to those around them. When we live under a government that limits what we are permitted to express, we inevitably face the frightening questions of where the line is drawn and who makes that decision. As Jewish females, we are prepared to defend the Nazi's right to march and express their views in our cities if that means that our own rights to free speech and, in turn, to free thought remain untouched.

9

Regulating Hate Speech Is Not Productive

Kenan Malik

Kenan Malik is a writer, lecturer, and broadcaster who founded Pandemonium, a website that promotes debate and upon which he publishes his writings and photography. Malik is the author of The Quest for a Moral Compass: A Global History of Ethics.

The alleged danger of restricting hate speech is expressed by Malik in the following interview-format article. He draws a line between defensible and indefensible speech, claiming that the former is often wrongly perceived as hateful and dangerous when it can be argued differently. Malik asserts that the impossibility of defining hate speech and distinguishing what is merely free expression from what is dangerous does not lessen bigotry, but rather weakens a free society.

I gave an interview last year to Peter Molnar for a book on the regulation of hate speech that he was editing with Michael Herz. The book comes out of a series of conferences and seminars organised by New York's Cardozo School of Law and the Central European University in Budapest. (I presented a paper at a seminar in Budapest). Other contributors include Jeremy Waldron, Ronald Dworkin, Kwame Anthony Appiah, Nadine Strossen and Bhikhu Parekh. The book is finally published this month under the

"Why Hate Speech Should Not Be Banned," by Kenan Malik, Kenan Malik, April 19, 2012. Reprinted by permission.

pithy title of *The Content and Context of Hate Speech: Rethinking Regulation and Responses.* And here is the interview.

Peter Molnar: Would you characterize some speech as 'hate speech', and do you think that it is possible to provide a reliable legal definition of 'hate speech'?

Kenan Malik: I am not sure that 'hate speech' is a particularly useful concept. Much is said and written, of course, that is designed to promote hatred. But it makes little sense to lump it all together in a single category, especially when hatred is such a contested concept.

In a sense, hate speech restriction has become a means not of addressing specific issues about intimidation or incitement, but of enforcing general social regulation. This is why if you look at hate speech laws across the world, there is no consistency about what constitutes hate speech. Britain bans abusive, insulting, and threatening speech. Denmark and Canada ban speech that is insulting and degrading. India and Israel ban speech that hurts religious feelings and incites racial and religious hatred. In Holland, it is a criminal offense deliberately to insult a particular group. Australia prohibits speech that offends, insults, humiliates, or intimidates individuals or groups. Germany bans speech that violates the dignity of, or maliciously degrades or defames, a group. And so on. In each case, the law defines hate speech in a different way.

One response might be to say: Let us define hate speech much more tightly. I think, however, that the problem runs much deeper. Hate speech restriction is a means not of tackling bigotry but of rebranding certain, often obnoxious, ideas or arguments as immoral. It is a way of making certain ideas illegitimate without bothering politically to challenge them. And that is dangerous.

PM: Setting aside legal restrictions, would you differentiate between claims (that target certain groups) that should be challenged in political debate and claims (that also target certain groups) that should be simply rejected as so immoral that they

don't deserve an answer other than the strongest rejection and moral condemnation?

KM: There are certainly claims that are so outrageous that one would not wish to waste one's time refuting them. If someone were to suggest that all Muslims should be tortured because they are potential terrorists, or that rape is acceptable, then clearly no rational argument will ever change their mind, or that of anyone who accepts such claims.

Much of what we call hate speech consists, however, of claims that may be contemptible but yet are accepted by many as morally defensible. Hence I am wary of the argument that some sentiments are so immoral they can simply be condemned without being contested. First, such blanket condemnations are often a cover for the inability or unwillingness politically to challenge obnoxious sentiments. Second, in challenging obnoxious sentiments, we are not simply challenging those who spout such views; we are also challenging the potential audience for such views. Dismissing obnoxious or hateful views as not worthy of response may not be the best way of engaging with such an audience. Whether or not an obnoxious claim requires a reply depends, therefore, not simply on the nature of the claim itself, but also on the potential audience for that claim.

PM: What do you think about proposals for restricting defamation of religion?

KM: It is as idiotic to imagine that one could defame religion as it is to imagine that one could defame politics or literature. Or that the Bible or the Qur'an should not be criticized or ridiculed in the same way as one might criticize or ridicule The Communist Manifesto or On the Origin of Species or Dante's Inferno.

A religion is, in part, a set of beliefs – about the world, its origins, and humanity's place in it – and a set of values that supposedly derive from those beliefs. Those beliefs and values should be treated no differently to any other sets of beliefs, and values that derive from them. I can be hateful of conservatism or communism. It should be open to me to be equally hateful of Islam and Christianity.

Proponents of religious defamation laws suggest that religion is not just a set of beliefs but an identity, and an exceptionally deeply felt one at that. It is true that religions often form deep-seated identities. But, then, so do many other beliefs. Communists were often wedded to their ideas even unto death. Many racists have an almost visceral attachment to their beliefs. Should I indulge them because their views are so deeply held? And while I do not see my humanism as an identity with a big 'I', I would challenge any Christian or Muslim to demonstrate that my beliefs are less deeply held than theirs.

Freedom of worship – including the freedom of believers to believe as they wish and to preach as they wish – should be protected. Beyond that, religion should have no privileges. Freedom of worship is, in a sense, another form of freedom of expression – the freedom to believe as one likes about the divine and to assemble and enact rituals with respect to those beliefs. You cannot protect freedom of worship, in other words, without protecting freedom of expression. Take, for instance, Geert Wilders' attempt to outlaw the Qur'an in Holland because it 'promotes hatred'. Or the investigation by the British police a few years ago of Iqbal Sacranie, former head of the Muslim Council of Britain, for derogatory comments he made about homosexuality. Both are examples of the way that defense of freedom of religion is inextricably linked with defense of freedom of speech. Or, to put it another way, in both cases, had the authorities been allowed to restrict freedom of expression, it would have had a devastating impact on freedom of worship. That is why the attempt to restrict defamation of religion is, ironically, an attack not just on freedom of speech but on freedom of worship too – and not least because one religion necessarily defames another. Islam denies the divinity of Christ, Christianity refuses to accept the Qur'an as the word of God. Each Holy Book blasphemes against the others.

One of the ironies of the current Muslim campaign for a law against religious defamation is that had such a law existed in the seventh century, Islam itself would never have been born. The creation of the faith was shocking and offensive to the adherents of the pagan religions out of which it grew, and equally so to the two other monotheistic religions of the age, Judaism and Christianity. Had seventh-century versions of today's religious censors had their way, the twenty-first-century versions may still have been fulminating against offensive speech, but it certainly would not have been Islam that was being offended.

At the heart of the debate about defamation of religion are actually not questions of faith or hatred, but of political power. Demanding that certain things cannot be said, whether in the name of respecting faith or of not offending cultures, is a means of defending the power of those who claim legitimacy in the name of that faith or that culture. It is a means of suppressing dissent, not from outside, but from within. What is often called offense to a community or a faith is actually a debate within that community or faith. In accepting that certain things cannot be said because they are offensive or hateful, those who wish to restrict free speech are simply siding with one side in such debates – and usually the more conservative, reactionary side.

PM: Do you support content-based bans of 'hate speech' through the criminal law, or do you instead agree with the American and Hungarian approach, which permits prohibition only of speech that creates imminent danger?

KM: I believe that no speech should be banned solely because of its content; I would distinguish 'content-based' regulation from 'effects-based' regulation and permit the prohibition only of speech that creates imminent danger. I oppose content-based bans both as a matter of principle and with a mind to the practical impact of such bans. Such laws are wrong in principle because free speech for everyone except bigots is not free speech at all. It is meaningless to defend the right of free expression for people with whose views we agree. The right to free speech only has political bite when we are forced to defend the rights of people with whose views we profoundly disagree.

And in practice, you cannot reduce or eliminate bigotry simply by banning it. You simply let the sentiments fester underground. As Milton once put it, to keep out 'evil doctrine' by licensing is 'like the exploit of that gallant man who thought to pound up the crows by shutting his Park-gate'.

Take Britain. In 1965, Britain prohibited incitement to racial hatred as part of its Race Relations Act. The following decade was probably the most racist in British history. It was the decade of 'Paki-bashing', when racist thugs would seek out Asians to beat up. It was a decade of firebombings, stabbings, and murders. In the early 1980s, I was organizing street patrols in East London to protect Asian families from racist attacks.

Nor were thugs the only problem. Racism was woven into the fabric of public institutions. The police, immigration officials – all were openly racist. In the twenty years between 1969 and 1989, no fewer than thirty-seven blacks and Asians were killed in police custody – almost one every six months. The same number again died in prisons or in hospital custody. When in 1982, cadets at the national police academy were asked to write essays about immigrants, one wrote, 'Wogs, nignogs and Pakis come into Britain take up our homes, our jobs and our resources and contribute relatively less to our once glorious country. They are, by nature, unintelligent. And can't at all be educated sufficiently to live in a civilised society of the Western world'. Another wrote that 'all blacks are pains and should be ejected from society'. So much for incitement laws helping create a more tolerant society.

Today, Britain is a very different place. Racism has not disappeared, nor have racist attacks, but the open, vicious, visceral bigotry that disfigured the Britain when I was growing up has largely ebbed away. It has done so not because of laws banning racial hatred but because of broader social changes and because minorities themselves stood up to the bigotry and fought back.

Of course, as the British experience shows, hatred exists not just in speech but also has physical consequences. Is it not important, critics of my view ask, to limit the fomenting of hatred to protect the lives of those who may be attacked? In asking this very question, they are revealing the distinction between speech and action. Saying something is not the same as doing it. But, in these post-ideological, postmodern times, it has become very unfashionable to insist on such a distinction.

In blurring the distinction between speech and action, what is really being blurred is the idea of human agency and of moral responsibility. Because lurking underneath the argument is the idea that people respond like automata to words or images. But people are not like robots. They think and reason and act on their thoughts and reasoning. Words certainly have an impact on the real world, but that impact is mediated through human agency.

Racists are, of course, influenced by racist talk. It is they, however, who bear responsibility for translating racist talk into racist action. Ironically, for all the talk of using free speech responsibly, the real consequence of the demand for censorship is to moderate the responsibility of individuals for their actions.

Having said that, there are clearly circumstances in which there is a direct connection between speech and action, where someone's words have directly led to someone else taking action. Such incitement should be illegal, but it has to be tightly defined. There has to be both a direct link between speech and action and intent on the part of the speaker for that particular act of violence to be carried out. Incitement to violence in the context of hate speech should be as tightly defined as in ordinary criminal cases. In ordinary criminal cases, incitement is, rightly, difficult legally to prove. The threshold for liability should not be lowered just because hate speech is involved.

PM: How tightly should we define the connection between incitement and the imminent danger of action? What about racist slogans in a soccer stadium, and imminent danger of violence on the crowded streets after the end of the game?

KM: Racist slogans, like any racist speech, should be a moral issue, not a legal one. If supporters are clearly set to attack others, or are directly inciting others to do so, then, of course, it becomes a matter for the law.

PM: What about this example: At the gay pride parade in Budapest, peaceful marchers were attacked. Some onlookers merely shouted homophobic statements; others, no doubt encouraged by the taunting, threw eggs and rocks at the marchers. If the hecklers later stated that they had not intended to incite violence, should they be subject to punishment or liability?

KM: Such questions cannot be answered in the abstract; it depends on the context. I would need to know more factual details than you have provided. If the two groups you mention were independent of each other and happened to turn up at the gay march at the same time, and if the perpetrators of violence would have attacked the marchers anyway, then I don't see that the non-violent homophobes have a legal case to answer. The non-violent homophobes are no more responsible for the violence of the violent homophobes in those circumstances than peaceful anti-globalization protestors are responsible for the actions of fellow-protestors who trash Starbucks or set cars alight.

If, on the other hand, there was a relationship between the two groups, or if the one was clearly egging on the other, and if without such encouragement the violent protestors would not have been violent, then, yes, there may well be a case to answer.

PM: What if the two groups of anti-globalization protestors are not independent from each other, if they belong to the same group, just some/most of them are peacefully shouting slogans, while others are acting violently? Would you draw a line between slogans – uttered without violence – that are hateful and slogans that might be angry but do not incite hatred?

KM: People should have the legal right to shout slogans, even hateful ones, and even though we might morally despise them for doing so. The law should deal with people acting violently, or those that directly incite others to violence. To 'incite hatred', as you put it, should not, of itself, be a criminal offence; the distinction is again between a particular attitude and a particular action.

PM: In that case, suppose the action is not violence but discrimination. That is, should it be only the imminent danger of violence that can justify restriction to speech, or does the imminent danger of discrimination suffice?

KM: I support laws against discrimination in the public sphere. But I absolutely oppose laws against the advocacy of discrimination. Equality is a political concept, and one to which I subscribe. But many people don't. It is clearly a highly contested concept. Should there be continued Muslim immigration into Europe? Should indigenous workers get priority in social housing? Should gays be allowed to adopt? These are all questions being keenly debated at the moment. I have strong views on all these issues, based on my belief in equality. But it would be absurd to suggest that only people who hold my kind of views should be able to advocate them. I find arguments against Muslim immigration, against equal access to housing, against gay adoptions unpalatable. But I accept that these are legitimate political arguments. A society that outlawed such arguments would, in my mind, be as reactionary as one that banned Muslim immigration or denied gays rights.

PM: But what about advocacy of discrimination that creates imminent danger of discrimination? For example, when members of a minority group would like to enter a restaurant or a bar and someone vehemently tells the security guard at the door that those people should not be allowed in.

KM: An individual who advocates such discrimination may be morally despicable but should not be held to have committed a legal offense. The security guard, however, and the establishment that so discriminates should be answerable to the law.

PM: Do you think that we can find a universal approach to criminal law restriction to incitement to hatred? Or should the regulation depend on the cultural context, and if so, in what way regulation could be different?

KM: I believe that free speech is a universal good and that all human societies best flourish with the greatest extension of free speech. It is often said, for example, even by free-speech advocates, that there is a case for Germany banning Holocaust denial. I don't accept that. Even in Germany – especially in Germany – what is needed is an open and robust debate on this issue.

PM: Would you suggest the same for Rwanda?

KM: Yes I would. What Rwanda requires is not the suppression of the deep-seated animosities but the ability of people openly to debate their differences. It's worth adding, given the argument for state regulation of hate speech, that in Rwanda it was the state that promoted the hatred that led to such devastating consequences.

PM: What would imminent danger caused by incitement to hatred mean in such an environment? In other words: Do you think that the legal concept of this imminence of danger can be contextual?

KM: The meaning of 'imminent danger' clearly depends upon circumstances. What constitutes imminent danger in, say, London or New York, where there exists a relatively stable, relatively liberal society, and a fairly robust framework of law and order, may be different from what constitutes imminent danger in Kigali or even in Moscow. And the meaning of imminent danger for a Jew in Berlin in 1936 was clearly different from that for a Jew – or a Muslim – in Berlin 2011. At the same time, in those times and in those societies in which particular groups are being made targets of intense hostility, this debate becomes almost irrelevant. In a climate of extreme hatred, as in Rwanda in 1994, or in Germany in the 1930s, it may be easier to incite people into harming others. But in such a climate, the niceties of what legally constitutes "imminent harm" would, and should, be the least of our worries. What would matter would be to confront such hatred and prejudice head on, both politically and physically.

What I am wary of is that in accepting the commonsense view that what constitutes danger is dependent on circumstances, we should not make the concept so elastic as to render it meaningless. Whether in London, New York, Berlin, or Kigali, speech should only be curtailed if such speech directly incites an act that causes or could cause physical harm to others and if individuals are in imminent danger of such harm because of those words. What is contextual is that in different circumstances, different kinds of speech could potentially place individuals in the way of such harm.

PM: Do you think that violent acts committed by hateful motivation deserve stricter punishments?

KM: I accept that intentions are not just morally but also legally relevant, and that different intentions can result in the imposition of different sentences. But when we make a distinction between, say, murder and manslaughter, we are making a distinction based on the kind or degree of harm the perpetrator intended. When it is suggested, however, that a racist murderer should receive a greater punishment than a non-racist murderer, a different kind of distinction is being drawn. The distinction here is not between the degrees of harm intended – in both cases the killer intended to kill – but between the thoughts that were in the minds of the respective killers. The distinction is between someone who might be thinking, 'I am going to kill you because I hate you because you looked at me the wrong way' and someone who might be thinking 'I am going to kill you because I hate you because you are black'. What is being criminalized here is simply a thought. And I am opposed to the category of thought crimes. Racist thoughts are morally offensive. But they should not be made a criminal offense.

Proponents argue that raising the punishment for hate crimes will (1) protect those who are abused or attacked simply because they belong to a particular group, and (2) send a message about the kind of society we wish to promote. But that is not fundamentally different from the argument for the criminalization of hate speech. And I am opposed to it for the same reason that I am opposed to the criminalization of hate speech.

PM: But does it not make a substantial difference that one might be able to avoid being attacked by not looking at her/his potential attackers the wrong way, while one cannot change her/his skin color?

KM: To the victim, such a distinction is, of course, of little comfort. There is also an implication here that some victims cannot help being victims, while others could, by having behaved differently, have avoided their misfortune. While this is not the same as suggesting that some victims ask to be victims, it is moving in that direction, and we should be careful about how far down this road we go.

The real issue remains the same: Should murderers with racist intent be punished to a greater degree than those with other kinds of malicious intent? I accept that racism is a pernicious social evil that needs specifically to be combated. But I reject the idea that we can, and should, combat racism by outlawing racist thoughts. If you accept, as I do, that thoughts in themselves – even racist thoughts – should not be legally prohibited, then you have to accept that a racist thought that leads to murder should not be seen as legally different from a nonracist thought that leads to murder.

PM: How, in your view, could we improve the social (non-legal) responses to 'hate speech'?

KM: The whole point of free speech is to create the conditions for robust debate, to be able to challenge obnoxious views. To argue for free speech but not to utilize it to challenge obnoxious, odious, and hateful views seems to me immoral. It is morally incumbent on those who argue for free speech to stand up to racism and bigotry.

At the same time, however, we should be clear that what often legitimizes bigotry are the arguments not of the bigots but of mainstream politicians and intellectuals who denounce bigotry and yet accept bigoted claims. Throughout Europe, mainstream politicians have denounced the rise of the far right. And throughout Europe, mainstream politicians have adapted to far-right arguments, clamping down on immigration, pursuing anti-Muslim measures, and so on. They have sometimes even adopted the language. In his first speech at the Labour Party conference after gaining the top office, former British Prime Minister Gordon Brown talked of ensuring 'British jobs for British workers', a slogan first popularized by the neofascist National Front. The National Front had twinned it with a second slogan: 'Three million blacks. Three million unemployed. Kick the blacks out'. Gordon Brown was, of course, not guilty of hate speech. But his use of that phrase probably did far more to promote xenophobic sentiment than any amount of "hate speech" by far-right bigots. Challenging bigotry requires us to challenge the mainstream ideas that give it sustenance, and to campaign against those discriminatory social practices and laws that help make the arguments of the racists, the sexists, and the homophobes more acceptable.

PM: Do you think that banning "hate speech" undermines, or at least weakens, the legitimacy of a democracy?

KM: Free speech and democracy are intimately linked. Without free speech there is no democracy. That is why any restriction on speech must be kept to the absolute minimum.

There are two ways in which banning hate speech undermines democracy. First, democracy can only work if every citizen believes that their voice counts. That however outlandish, outrageous, or obnoxious one's belief may be, they nevertheless have the right to express it and to try to win support for it. When people feel they no longer possess that right, then democracy itself suffers, as does the legitimacy of those in power.

Not just the banning of hate speech but the very categorization of an argument or a sentiment as 'hate speech' can be problematic for the democratic process. I am in no doubt that some speech is designed to promote hatred. And I accept that certain arguments –

like the direct incitement of violence – should indeed be unlawful. But the category 'hate speech' has come to function quite differently from prohibitions on incitement to violence. It has become a means of rebranding obnoxious political arguments as immoral and so beyond the boundaries of accepted reasonable debate. It makes certain sentiments illegitimate, thereby disenfranchising those who hold such views.

And this brings me to the second point as to why the banning of hate speech undermines democracy. Branding an opinion as 'hate speech' does not simply disenfranchise those holding such a view; it also absolves the rest of us of the responsibility of politically challenging it. Where once we might have challenged obnoxious or hateful sentiments politically, today we are more likely simply to seek to outlaw them.

In 2007, James Watson, the codiscoverer of the structure of DNA, claimed of Africans that their 'intelligence is not the same as ours' and that blacks are genetically intellectually inferior. He was rightly condemned for his arguments. But most of those who condemned him did not bother challenging the arguments, empirically or politically. They simply insisted that it is morally unacceptable to imagine that blacks are intellectually inferior. Britain's Equality and Human Rights Commission studied the remarks to see if it could bring any legal action. London's Science Museum, at which Watson was to have delivered a lecture, canceled his appearance, claiming that the Nobel Laureate had 'gone beyond the point of acceptable debate.' New York's Cold Spring Harbor Laboratory, of which Watson was director, not only disowned Watson's remarks but forced him eventually to resign.

I fundamentally disagree with Watson. Indeed I have written more than one book challenging such ideas, and have many times publicly debated their supporters. But I also think that it was as legitimate for Watson to have expressed his opinion as it is for me to express mine, even if I believe his assertion was factually wrong, morally suspect, and politically offensive. Simply to dismiss

Watson's claim as beyond the bounds of reasonable debate is to refuse to confront the actual arguments, to decline to engage with an idea that clearly has considerable purchase, and therefore to do disservice to democracy.

10

It Can Be Difficult to Distinguish "Fighting Words"

David L. Hudson Jr.

David L. Hudson Jr. specializes in First Amendment issues. He writes for the First Amendment Center, as well as other publications. He teaches law and served as a scholar at the First Amendment Center. He also authored or co-authored books about the U.S. Supreme Court, the Constitution, and student rights.

The only recent barrier between legality and unlimited free speech in the United States has been the establishment — through the Supreme Court — of "fighting words," which stipulate that hate speech which incites violence must be prohibited. The author of this article, who serves as an expert on First Amendment rights, explains in detail what the term "fighting words" covers and how it will shape the free speech/hate speech debate for years to come.

An angry individual unleashes a torrent of profanity upon a police officer. The officer tries to remain calm and ignore the enraged individual. But the profanity does not stop with one curse word, and the officer arrests the person for disorderly conduct or breach of the peace.

The individual contends that the officer violated his First Amendment right to free speech, which includes the right to engage in offensive expression. The individual asserts he has the right to

"Fighting Words," by David L. Hudson Jr., First Amendment Center, July 2009. Reprinted in full, with permission, Newseum Institute, 2017.

criticize government officials — one of the central rights the First Amendment is designed to protect. The government counters that the individual has no First Amendment protection because he has uttered "fighting words" — an unprotected category of speech. Freedom of speech is not advanced, the government asserts, by a stream of profanities with little or no intellectual substance.

Who should prevail in such a situation? Can the government constitutionally punish an individual for expressing himself in an offensive and uncivil manner? Does it matter whether the recipient of the profane outburst is a police officer?

These cases arise in two basic postures. In the first type of case, an individual faces criminal charges for disorderly conduct based on obnoxious, offensive speech and attempts to make a First Amendment-based defense. The question becomes whether the individual's speech constituted unprotected "fighting words" or protected free speech.

In the second type, criminal charges are dropped against the individual, who then files a civil rights lawsuit alleging a violation of his First Amendment free-speech rights. He or she contends that the police violated his or her free-speech rights because they punished him (in the form of an arrest and perhaps criminal charges) for protected speech. The police counter that the individual engaged in fighting words and that the police should receive qualified immunity because a reasonable police officer in that situation would not know whether the individual's speech constituted fighting words or protected speech.

Qualified immunity is a doctrine that shields government officials from liability when they do not violate clearly established constitutional or statutory law. If it is unclear whether an individual engaged in fighting words, the governmental official may receive qualified immunity even if the official wrongly assumes the individual uttered fighting words.

These hypothetical situations form the basis for a surprisingly complex area of First Amendment jurisprudence. The First Amendment protects a wide range of expression that many people do not like. Former U.S. Supreme Court Justice William Brennan wrote in the Court's 1989 decision in *Texas v. Johnson*: "If there is a bedrock principle underlying the First Amendment, it is that government may not prohibit the expression of an idea simply because it finds it offensive or disagreeable."

But the Supreme Court has ruled that certain offensive words — called "fighting words" — can be prohibited. The genesis of the high court's fighting-words jurisprudence began with the 1942 decision *Chaplinsky v. New Hampshire.*

Origins of the Fighting-Words Doctrine

The Supreme Court first developed the fighting-words doctrine in the case of Walter Chaplinsky in 1942. Chaplinsky, a Jehovah's Witness, was distributing religious literature on the streets of Rochester, N.H.

Apparently, several citizens complained about Chaplinsky's comments. Some alleged that he was denouncing all religion as a "racket." A city marshal named Bowering confronted Chaplinsky and warned him that people were getting restless with his activities.

Chaplinsky then allegedly said to Bowering: "You are a God damned racketeer" and "a damned Fascist and the whole government of Rochester are Fascists or agents of Fascists."

Chaplinsky was charged and convicted under a city ordinance that prohibited people in public from calling others they encountered "any offensive or derisive name." Chaplinsky claimed that the city law violated the First Amendment.

The Supreme Court disagreed in its unanimous opinion in Chaplinsky v. New Hampshire, writing:

> It is well understood that the right of free speech is not absolute at all times and under all circumstances. There are certain well-defined and narrowly limited classes of speech, the prevention and punishment of which has never been thought to raise any Constitutional problem. These include the lewd and obscene, the profane, the libelous, and the insulting or "fighting" words — those which by their very utterance inflict injury or tend to incite

an immediate breach of the peace. It has been well observed that such utterances are no essential part of any exposition of ideas, and are of such slight social value as a step to truth that any benefit may be derived from them is clearly outweighed by the social interest in order and morality. "Resort to epithets or personal abuse is not in any proper sense communication of information or opinion safeguarded by the Constitution, and its punishment as a criminal act would raise no question under that instrument."

The Court noted that the state high court had limited the construction of the city law to apply only to those "face-to-face words" or "epithets likely to provoke the average person to retaliation and thereby cause a breach of the peace."

Chaplinsky also argued that applying the statute to him violated the First Amendment because the state had not shown that the epithets he used were true "fighting words." The Court rejected that argument, writing that "argument is unnecessary to demonstrate that the appellations 'damn racketeer' and 'damn Fascist' are epithets likely to provoke the average person to retaliation, and thereby cause a breach of the peace."

Although the Court seemingly curtailed the fighting-words doctrine in later decisions, it has never overruled the Chaplinsky decision, so it remains in effect.

Free-speech expert Robert O'Neil, in his Law and Contemporary Problems article "Rights in Conflict: The First Amendment's Third Century," writes that "the Chaplinsky decision has caused no end of confusion during the ensuing six decades."

Limiting Fighting-Words Doctrine

In a series of decisions, the Court limited the fighting-words doctrine expressed in Chaplinsky. Before the end of the decade, the U.S. Supreme Court gave First Amendment protection to a controversial speaker in Terminiello v. City of Chicago. Arthur Terminiello, an ex-Catholic priest, was charged with disorderly conduct after he gave a racist, anti-Semitic speech in a Chicago auditorium to the Christian Veterans of America.

More than a thousand people were outside the auditorium gathering in protest of the meeting. Terminiello criticized the protesters and then criticized various political and racial groups.

Local police charged him with breach of the peace, defined by the trial court as any "misbehavior which violates the public peace and decorum." The trial court instructed the jury that "misbehavior may constitute a breach of the peace if it stirs the public to anger, invites dispute, brings about a condition of unrest, or creates a disturbance."

City officials argued that Terminiello could be punished because his speech constituted fighting words. The city's argument carried the day in a state trial court and two state appeals courts. However, in May 1949, the U.S. Supreme Court overturned the conviction by a 5-4 vote. Writing for the majority, Justice William Douglas noted that the lower courts had analyzed the issue as whether the speech constituted fighting words under Chaplinsky.

However, Douglas decided the case on the overly broad nature of the jury instructions. In one of the most cited passages in First Amendment jurisprudence, Douglas wrote:

> Accordingly, a function of free speech under our system of government is to invite dispute. It may indeed serve its high purpose when it induces a condition of unrest, creates dissatisfaction with conditions as they are, or even stirs people to anger. Speech is often provocative and challenging. It may strike at prejudices and preconceptions and have profound unsettling effects as it presses for acceptance of an idea.

Douglas concluded that a conviction could not stand on a jury instruction that permitted the punishment of a speaker for speech that invited public dispute. He rejected the argument that the statute only punished unprotected fighting words. "Petitioner was not convicted under a statute so narrowly construed," the court wrote. "For all anyone knows he [Terminiello] was convicted under the parts of the ordinance (as construed) which, for example, make it an offense merely to invite dispute or to bring about a condition of unrest."

In several later decisions, the Court continued to limit when individuals could be punished for uttering offensive language. For example, the high court ruled in Cohen v. California (1971) that an individual could not be criminally prosecuted for wearing a jacket bearing the words "Fuck the Draft" into a courthouse.

Officials charged Paul Cohen with violating a California law prohibiting "maliciously and willfully disturbing the peace or quiet of any neighborhood or person by … offensive conduct."

The state argued that Cohen's jacket constituted fighting words under Chaplinsky. The Supreme Court disagreed, writing in its 1971 ruling that the words on the jacket were not a "direct personal insult" and that no one had reacted violently to the jacket.

In oft-cited language, Justice John Paul Harlan wrote:

> "For while the particular four-letter word being litigated here is perhaps more distasteful than most others of its genre, it is nevertheless often true that one man's vulgarity is another's lyric. Indeed, we think it is largely because governmental officials cannot make principled distinctions in this area that the Constitution leaves manners of taste and style so largely to the individual."

This ruling established that fighting words should be confined to direct personal insults.

O'Neil questions whether the Chaplinsky and Cohen decisions can be reconciled: "Cohen and Chaplinsky cannot coexist indefinitely, because one [Chaplinsky] declares that offensive epithets are 'no essential part of any exposition of ideas' while the other insists with equal conviction that 'one man's vulgarity is another's lyric.'"

A year after Cohen, the Supreme Court struck down the conviction of a defendant under a Georgia breach-of-the-peace law in Gooding v. Wilson. James Wilson told a police officer: "White son of a bitch, I'll kill you," and "You son of a bitch, I'll choke you to death." For these words, Wilson was arrested and convicted of disorderly conduct.

He was charged under a statute that defined disorderly conduct as follows: "Any person who shall, without provocation, use to or of another, and in his presence … opprobrious words or abusive language, tending to cause a breach of the peace … shall be guilty of a misdemeanor."

The state argued that the statute was constitutional because it only applied to "fighting words." However, the U.S. Supreme Court reversed the conviction, finding that the statute punished more than fighting words as defined under Chaplinsky.

The Court first examined the language of the statute. "The dictionary definitions of 'opprobrious' and 'abusive' give them greater reach than 'fighting' words," Supreme Court Justice William Brennan wrote for the majority. The court also noted that other Georgia courts had interpreted the statute to apply to more than fighting words.

The Court reached a similar result in 1974 in *Lewis v. City of New Orleans*. Mallie Lewis was convicted under a city law which prohibited using "obscene or opprobrious language" to police officers. Lewis was arrested after she yelled obscenities at a police officer who asked her husband to produce his driver's license.

Justice Brennan determined that this law infringed on First Amendment freedoms because it was not confined to fighting words. He reasoned that "the proscription of the use of 'opprobrious language,' embraces words that do not 'by their very utterance inflict injury or tend to incite an immediate breach of the peace.'" Brennan ruled that the Louisiana Supreme Court had failed to confine the statute to just fighting words.

The Court again struck down the conviction of an individual for making offensive comments to a police officer in 1987 in *City of Houston v. Hill*, Raymond Wayne Hill was arrested after he yelled at a police officer who was questioning his friend. Hill said to the officer: "Why don't you pick on somebody your own size?"

The officer arrested Hill for violating a city law prohibiting a person from opposing, molesting or abusing, or interrupting a police officer during his duties.

After Hill was acquitted in municipal court, he filed a civil rights lawsuit. In his lawsuit, he asked that the federal courts declare the ordinance unconstitutional. The case eventually reached the U.S. Supreme Court which sided with Hill. Before the high court, the city argued that the ordinance prohibited "core criminal conduct."

The Supreme Court disagreed, finding that the ordinance dealt with speech. "Contrary to the city's contention, the First Amendment protects a significant amount of verbal criticism and challenge directed at police officers," Brennan wrote.

"The freedom of individuals verbally to oppose or challenge police action without thereby risking arrest is one of the principal characteristics by which we distinguish a free nation from a police state," Brennan wrote.

Brennan determined that the law was not narrowly tailored to prohibit disorderly conduct or fighting words. The court concluded that the ordinance "criminalizes a substantial amount of constitutionally protected speech, and accords the police unconstitutional discretion in enforcement."

As a result of these Supreme Court decisions, many state and local governments have amended their statutes to narrow significantly the range of verbal conduct that can be criminalized. Many state supreme courts have limited their laws to apply only to fighting words.

Much of the case law now centers on whether a person's speech qualifies as fighting words. The government tends to argue that the person was charged not for his speech, but for his conduct — flailing of arms or shouting of specific unprotected threats, for example.

In the 1992 cross-burning case of *R.A.V. v. City of St. Paul*, Justice Antonin Scalia wrote that "the exclusion of 'fighting words' from the scope of the First Amendment simply means that, for purposes of that Amendment, the unprotected features of the words are, despite their verbal character, essentially a 'nonspeech' element of communication." (The Court invalidated the cross-burning law because it selectively punished only a particular form of fighting words. Justice Scalia considered this to an example of unconstitutional viewpoint discrimination.)

Lower Courts in Disarray

The lower courts have had a difficult time determining whether certain epithets constitute "fighting words." At the very least, they have reached maddeningly inconsistent results. Consider the following situations in which offensive statements were found not to constitute fighting words:

- Calling a police officer a "son of a bitch" (Johnson v. Campbell, 3rd Circuit, 2003).
- Yelling "fuck you all" to a police officer and security personnel at a nightclub (Cornelius v. Brubaker, Minnesota District Court, 2003).
- Telling a police officer: "I'm tired of this God damned police sticking their nose in shit that doesn't even involve them" (Brendle v. City of Houston, Court of Appeals of the State of Mississippi, 2000).
- Telling a security officer "This is bullshit" when rousted from a parking lot (U.S. v. McDermott, Eastern District of Pennsylvania, 1997).

However, other courts have determined that the expressions in the following situations were fighting words:

- Flashing a sexually suggestive sign repeatedly to a young woman driving a car (State v. Hubbard, Minnesota Court of Appeals, 2001).
- Yelling racial slurs at two African-American women (In re John M., Arizona Court of Appeals, 2001).
- Repeatedly yelling the words "whore," "harlot" and "Jezebel" at a nude woman on the beach (Wisconsin v. Ovadal, Wisconsin Court of Appeals, 2003).

- Calling a police officer a "white, racist motherfucker" and wishing his mother would die (State v. Clay, Minnesota Court of Appeals, 1999).
- Calling a police officer a "fucking asshole" in a loud voice and attempting to spit on the officer (State v. York, Maine Supreme Judicial Court, 1999).

The different results reached in the lower courts, including the examples mentioned above, are difficult to explain. O'Neil writes that "much confusion surrounds the constitutional boundaries in the quest for civility." Generally, if an individual engages in any threatening conduct in addition to verbal assaults, a fighting-words charge is more likely to stick. Many courts will look at the full circumstances to see if profane or insulting language was accompanied by any threatening behavior or conduct.

Some courts find that police officers are held to a higher standard than other people if the angry speech is likely to lead to an immediate breach of the peace. For example, in its 2000 decision in *Martilla v. City of Lynchburg*, a Virginia appeals court wrote that "the First Amendment requires properly trained police officers to exercise a higher degree of restraint when confronted by disorderly conduct and abusive language." In other words, profanity or insults directed at police are less likely to be considered fighting words than if they were aimed at other people.

Supreme Court Justice Lewis Powell articulated this concern in his concurring opinion in *Lewis v. New Orleans*, when he wrote that "the situation may be different where such words are addressed to a police officer trained to exercise a higher degree of restraint than the average citizen."

Other courts have determined that the response of the recipient does not control whether expression qualifies as fighting words. For example, the Minnesota Court of Appeals wrote in its 1999 decision *State v. Clay*:

> "A defendant can be convicted for disorderly conduct based on the utterance of fighting words without the prosecution having to prove that violence actually resulted. The focus is properly

on the nature of the words and the circumstances in which they were spoken rather than on the actual response. The actual response of the addressee or object of the words is relevant, but not determinative, of the issue of whether the utterances meet the fighting words test." [*State v. Clay*, CX-99-343 (Minn. App.)(9/14/99), citing In re M.A.H., 572 N.W.2d 752 (Minn. App. 1997).]

Qualified Immunity

Another area of confusion in fighting-words cases stems from the use of the qualified-immunity defense. Recall that in many fighting-words cases, the question becomes whether a reasonable police officer should have known that he or she violated clearly established constitutional law in arresting an individual for disorderly conduct or breach of the peace partly because of the person's profane or insulting language.

If the case law in a particular jurisdiction is divided on the fighting-words question, a reviewing court may grant the officer qualified immunity. In Purtell v. Mason (2008), a three-judge panel of the 7th Circuit considered the question of qualified immunity and fighting words in an unusual case involving a suburban Chicago man who erected tombstones with his neighbors' names and insulting messages on them. Police officer Bruce Mason arrested Jeffrey Purtell, claiming that the messages on his tombstone qualified as fighting words. Purtell sued Mason, alleging that his free-speech rights had been violated. Mason countered that he was entitled to qualified immunity because any reasonable officer would have thought that the words on the tombstones were fighting words.

The 7th Circuit panel ruled that the tombstone messages did not qualify as fighting words because they "were not, in context, the sort of provocatively abusive speech that inherently tends to incite an immediate breach of the peace." However, the panel also granted the Mason qualified immunity, writing that the officer's "mistake in thinking he could constitutionally order Purtell to dismantle the tombstone display on pain of arrest was one a reasonable officer might make in this situation." The panel concluded: "First Amendment line-drawing is often difficult, even in hindsight."

The U.S. Supreme Court issued an opinion in 2009 on qualified immunity that changed the equation in constitutional law cases. Previously, in considering qualified immunity, a court — as the 7th Circuit did in Purtell — first had to determine whether there was a constitutional violation. Then the court would consider whether the law was clearly established. But in Pearson v. Callahan (2009), the Supreme Court ruled that judges can decide the "clearly established" question first without having to tackle the often-difficult question of whether there was a constitutional violation.

In the fighting-words context, this means that a reviewing court might skip over the question of whether certain profane or insulting speech constituted fighting words and simply rule that an officer did not violate clearly established law.

The varying decisions in the lower courts — and the complexity of the qualified-immunity doctrine — show that judges struggle with whether profane speech crosses the line from protected criticism or protected expression into the realm of unprotected fighting words. As Justice Harlan wrote in his Cohen opinion: "This case may seem at first blush too inconsequential to find its way into our books, but the issue it presents is of no small constitutional significance." Whether expression constitutes fighting words, remains a difficult, contentious issue that is also of "no small constitutional significance."

11

There Is No "Hate Speech" Exception to the First Amendment

Eugene Volokh

Eugene Volokh teaches free speech law and other related subjects at the UCLA School of Law. He previously clerked for Supreme Court Justice Sandra Day O'Connor. Volokh has also authored several textbooks, including one about the First Amendment.

This legal expert claims that the narrow exceptions to the virtually limitless free speech allowed by the First Amendment do not include hate speech. He does not tie "fighting words" specifically to hate speech, citing differences between the two, and says he believes that those seeking to legally place limits on hate speech should abandon the simple argument that hate speech is not free speech. Volokh argues that the First Amendment as currently constituted allows one to disparage others based on race, religion, gender, or sexual orientation.

I keep hearing about a supposed "hate speech" exception to the First Amendment, or statements such as, "This isn't free speech, it's hate speech," or "When does free speech stop and hate speech begin?" But there is no hate speech exception to the First Amendment. Hateful ideas (whatever exactly that might mean) are just as protected under the First Amendment as other ideas. One is as free to condemn Islam—or Muslims, or Jews, or blacks,

"No, There's No 'Hate Speech' Exception to the First Amendment," by Eugene Volokh, The Washington Post, May 7, 2015. Reprinted by permission.

or whites, or illegal aliens, or native-born citizens—as one is to condemn capitalism or Socialism or Democrats or Republicans.

To be sure, there are some kinds of speech that are unprotected by the First Amendment. But those narrow exceptions have nothing to do with "hate speech" in any conventionally used sense of the term. For instance, there is an exception for "fighting words" —face-to-face personal insults addressed to a specific person, of the sort that are likely to start an immediate fight. But this exception isn't limited to racial or religious insults, nor does it cover all racially or religiously offensive statements. Indeed, when the City of St. Paul tried to specifically punish bigoted fighting words, the Supreme Court held that this selective prohibition was unconstitutional (R.A.V. v. City of St. Paul (1992)), even though a broad ban on all fighting words would indeed be permissible. (And, notwithstanding CNN anchor Chris Cuomo's Tweet that "hate speech is excluded from protection," and his later claims that by "hate speech" he means "fighting words," the fighting words exception is not generally labeled a "hate speech" exception, and isn't coextensive with any established definition of "hate speech" that I know of.)

The same is true of the other narrow exceptions, such as for true threats of illegal conduct or incitement intended to and likely to produce imminent illegal conduct (i.e., illegal conduct in the next few hours or maybe days, as opposed to some illegal conduct some time in the future). Indeed, threatening to kill someone because he's black (or white), or intentionally inciting someone to a likely and immediate attack on someone because he's Muslim (or Christian or Jewish), can be made a crime. But this isn't because it's "hate speech"; it's because it's illegal to make true threats and incite imminent crimes against anyone and for any reason, for instance because they are police officers or capitalists or just someone who is sleeping with the speaker's ex-girlfriend.

The Supreme Court did, in Beauharnais v. Illinois (1952), uphold a "group libel" law that outlawed statements that expose racial or religious groups to contempt or hatred, unless the speaker could show that the statements were true, and were said with "good motives" and for "justifiable ends." But this too was treated by the Court as just a special case of a broader First Amendment exception—the one for libel generally. And Beauharnais is widely understood to no longer be good law, given the Court's restrictions on the libel exception. See New York Times Co. v. Sullivan (1964) (rejecting the view that libel is categorically unprotected, and holding that the libel exception requires a showing that the libelous accusations be "of and concerning" a particular person); Garrison v. Louisiana (1964) (generally rejecting the view that a defense of truth can be limited to speech that is said for "good motives" and for "justifiable ends"); Philadelphia Newspapers, Inc. v. Hepps (1986) (generally rejecting the view that the burden of proving truth can be placed on the defendant); R.A.V. v. City of St. Paul (1992) (holding that singling bigoted speech is unconstitutional, even when that speech fits within a First Amendment exception); Nuxoll ex rel. Nuxoll v. Indian Prairie Sch. Dist. # 204, 523 F.3d 668, 672 (7th Cir. 2008) (concluding that Beauharnais is no longer good law); Dworkin v. Hustler Magazine Inc., 867 F.2d 1188, 1200 (9th Cir. 1989) (likewise); Am. Booksellers Ass'n, Inc. v. Hudnut, 771 F.2d 323, 331 n.3 (7th Cir. 1985) (likewise); Collin v. Smith, 578 F.2d 1197, 1205 (7th Cir. 1978) (likewise); Tollett v. United States, 485 F.2d 1087, 1094 n.14 (8th Cir. 1973) (likewise); Erwin Chemerinsky, Constitutional Law: Principles and Policies 1043-45 (4th ed. 2011); Laurence Tribe, Constitutional Law, §12-17, at 926; Toni M. Massaro, Equality and Freedom of Expression: The Hate Speech Dilemma, 32 Wm. & Mary L. Rev. 211, 219 (1991); Robert C. Post, Cultural Heterogeneity and Law: Pornography, Blasphemy, and the First Amendment, 76 Calif. L. Rev. 297, 330-31 (1988).

Finally, "hostile environment harassment law" has sometimes been read as applying civil liability—or administrative discipline by universities—to allegedly bigoted speech in workplaces, universities, and places of public accommodation. There is a hot debate on whether those restrictions are indeed constitutional; they have generally been held unconstitutional when applied to universities, but decisions are mixed as to civil liability based on speech that creates hostile environments in workplaces (see the pages linked to at this site for more information on the subject). But even when those restrictions have been upheld, they have been justified precisely on the rationale that they do not criminalize speech (or otherwise punish it) in society at large, but only apply to particular contexts, such as workplaces. None of them represent a "hate speech" exception, nor have they been defined in terms of "hate speech."

For this very reason, "hate speech" also doesn't have any fixed legal meaning under U.S. law. U.S. law has just never had occasion to define "hate speech"—any more than it has had occasion to define rudeness, evil ideas, unpatriotic speech, or any other kind of speech that people might condemn but that does not constitute a legally relevant category.

Of course, one can certainly argue that First Amendment law should be changed to allow bans on hate speech (whether bigoted speech, blasphemy, blasphemy to which foreigners may respond with attacks on Americans or blasphemy or flag burning or anything else). Perhaps some statements of the "This isn't free speech, it's hate speech" variety are deliberate attempts to call for such an exception, though my sense is that they are usually (incorrect) claims that the exception already exists.

I think no such exception should be recognized, but of course, like all questions about what the law ought to be, this is a matter that can be debated. Indeed, people have a First Amendment right to call for speech restrictions, just as they have a First Amendment right to call for gun bans or bans on Islam or government-imposed race discrimination or anything else that current constitutional law forbids. Constitutional law is no more set in stone than any other law.

But those who want to make such arguments should acknowledge that they are calling for a change in First Amendment law, and should explain just what that change would be, so people can thoughtfully evaluate it. Calls for a new First Amendment exception for "hate speech" shouldn't just rely on the undefined term "hate speech"—they should explain just what viewpoints the government would be allowed to suppress, what viewpoints would remain protected, and how judges, juries, and prosecutors are supposed to distinguish the two. Saying "this isn't free speech, it's hate speech" doesn't, I think, suffice.

12

Hate Speech Is Harmful, but It Shouldn't Be Legislated

Joyce Arthur and Peter Tatchell

Joyce Arthur is an activist, feminist, and writer. Peter Tatchell is an advocate for human rights, particularly LGBTQ rights. The New Internationalist is an independent, not-profit media cooperative that has published magazines and books for more than 40 years. It specializes in investigative reporting about such subjects as human rights and politics, as well as social and environmental justice.

Joyce Arthur and Peter Tatchell voice their disagreement on the subject of hate speech as a potential crime in the following give-and-take article. Arthur sides with countries that have worked through legal channels to limit hate speech, citing other restrictions to free speech as well. Tatchell expresses his distaste for hate speech while defending its current legal status in the United States beyond that which clearly incites violence. He argues that the subjectivity of what constitutes hate speech makes it difficult to define and regulate.

Joyce

A consensus exists in most Western democracies on the legitimacy of using laws to punish or inhibit hate speech, in order to prevent hate crimes, provide redress to victims, support vulnerable groups, protect human rights, and promote values of equality and respect.

"Argument – Should Hate Speech Be a Crime?" by Joyce Arthur and Peter Tatchell, New Internationalist, December 1, 2012. https://newint.org/sections/argument/2012/12/01/is-hate-speech-crime-argument/. Licensed under CC BY-NC-ND 3.0 Unported.

Countries have international obligations to combat racism, which require enacting hate speech legislation. As in Canada, reasonable limits can be placed on freedom of expression to balance it against other fundamental rights, such as freedom from discrimination. Free speech is no sacred cow, anyway, since various restrictions are already accepted by society – for example, bans on threats, defamation, false advertising, noise around hospitals or schools.

While laws are only one tool among many to fight hate speech, they should at least be used against the most egregious cases. Courts and tribunals are capable of objectively weighing evidence and applying criteria to ensure that legitimate free speech or merely offensive speech are not captured.

Hate speech is dangerous because words have power and can influence others to act. The assassinations of abortion providers in the US prove that words do not have to incite violence explicitly to cause violence. Hate speech promotes division and intolerance; it harms and marginalizes the vulnerable groups it targets. Free speech is exercised largely by the privileged at the expense of the unprivileged who do not have a level ground on which to respond. Having no hate speech laws is unjust – as if people's dignity and human rights should be up for debate in the public square and 'may the best argument win'.

Peter

Hate speech is merely saying hateful things. It is not the same as discrimination, harassment, threats or violence – all of which are qualitatively worse and are rightly criminalized.

I don't approve of hate speech and believe it should be discouraged and challenged. However, I don't think it should be criminalized, unless it is expressed in a particularly aggressive, inflammatory or sustained manner, in which case it would amount to criminal threats or harassment.

One of the main problems with hate speech laws is defining what constitutes hate. Unlike incitement to violence, it is highly subjective. The line between hate speech and legitimate unpalatable viewpoints is hard to draw with certainty, clarity and consistency.

Several Christian and Muslim street preachers have been arrested in Britain for hate speech. Their crime? They said that homosexuality is immoral and that gay people will go to hell. I disagree with them but opposed their prosecution. What they were saying was hurtful but not hateful. They did not express their views in a bullying or menacing tone.

Free speech is one of the hallmarks of a democratic society. It should only be restricted in extreme, compelling circumstances. Criminalizing views that are objectionable and offensive is the slippery slope to censorship and to the closing down of open debate. It is also counter-productive. It risks making martyrs of people with bigoted opinions and deflects from the real solution to hate speech: education and rational debate. Hate speech should be protested and challenged, not criminalized.

Joyce

Hate speech is a public expression of discrimination against a vulnerable group (based on race, gender, sexual orientation, disability etc) and it is counter-productive not to criminalize it. A society that allows hate speech to go unpunished is one that tolerates discrimination and invites violence. Decades of hateful anti-abortion rhetoric in the US led to assassinations of providers, because hate speech is a precursor to violence.

Hate speech has no redeeming value, so we should never pretend it occupies a rightful spot in the marketplace of ideas, or has anything to do with 'rational debate'. Challenging hate speech through education and debate is not enough. Governments have a duty to protect citizens and reduce discrimination and violence by criminalizing hate speech.

Defining a crime with certainty, clarity and consistency is always a somewhat subjective exercise, but one that courts are expressly designed to do. Hate speech can be defined and prosecuted fairly without going down a slippery slope. An example is Canada's

'Taylor test' in which hate speech must express 'unusually strong and deep-felt emotions of detestation, calumny and vilification'.

Specific arrests or even prosecutions of hate speakers may not meet the test of criminal hate speech, and do not prove that hate speech laws are counter-productive. (In my view, however, only hate speakers with a wide audience or who engage in repeated ongoing hate speech should be prosecuted.) The justice system is a human institution and abuses can happen, but the answer is to refine and reform laws, not to scrap them.

Peter

I disagree that hate speech is an expression of discrimination. It's an expression of prejudice; not discrimination. Words and discrimination are two different things – unless the words explicitly incite unlawful discrimination; in which case they should be crimes because they incite criminal acts.

Mere hateful views shouldn't be criminal. Who decides what is hateful? The state should not have such power. It's open to abuse, as happened to anti-war protesters who abused British soldiers for their role in Iraq.

You suggest the police and courts are capable of distinguishing between hate speech and merely offensive speech. This is not true in Britain, where insults can be treated as hate speech. I was arrested for saying the homophobia and sexism of Islamist extremists is akin to the mentality of the Nazis. Separately, a youth was arrested for calling Scientology a dangerous cult. In both instances, it was deemed we had committed religious hate crimes.

Although it is claimed that hate speech influences people to commit hate violence, it's difficult to demonstrate that anyone has responded to hateful words with violent acts. The causal link is unproven. People don't kill abortion providers because they heard a hate speech. They commit these crimes because of a zealous belief that abortion is immoral.

I have some sympathy for your narrow definition of hate speech (the Taylor test) and that only repeated hate speech to a wide audience should be criminalized. Perhaps this is where we come close to common ground?

Joyce

In Canada, legal definitions of discrimination encompass hate speech.

I agree that people should not be arrested for the types of insults you describe. But one bad law or the abuse of laws is not an argument against hate speech laws. We are smart enough to craft better definitions of hate speech that protect marginalized groups from discrimination based only on immutable characteristics, which include religious affiliation but not specific religious beliefs or behaviours. Blasphemy must be permitted.

It can be very difficult to prove the causal effects of any law, but we accept living under a system of laws because they serve many other purposes. That said, a US court found that 'Wanted Posters' issued in the 1990s by anti-abortion groups for a dozen named abortion providers constituted a true threat because they led to the murders of several of them, even though the posters made no specific threats. People kill abortion providers not simply because they believe abortion is immoral, but because widespread hate speech against doctors creates an atmosphere of perceived acceptance and impunity for their actions.

Hate speech is destructive to society and to its victims. Enduring hatred over years can limit people's opportunities, isolate them socially, push them into poverty, lead to loss of self-esteem and depression, and endanger their health and safety. It is wrong to diminish the dignity and lives of some people just so others can freely spout hate against them. Leading purveyors of hate (at least) should be prosecuted.

Peter

I share your view that if a person is subjected to prolonged, extreme hatred it is damaging, wrong and should be criminalized. But this amounts to harassment and can be dealt with using anti-harassment laws, without the need for legislation against hate speech.

The abuse of abortion doctors is disgusting but I don't think it signals that it's okay to kill them. On the contrary, since murder is a criminal offence with severe penalties, society signals that killing doctors is impermissible. The 'Wanted' posters you describe were more than hate speech. They were de facto incitements to murder, which is rightly a crime.

We both agree that hate speech is a bad thing. We differ on how to tackle it. Hate speech laws address a problem after it has happened. I'd prefer to eradicate hate before it's expressed. Suppressing hate speech by use of the criminal law is, at best, a short-term fix. A better solution is education against hateful ideas.

I'd like to see compulsory school lessons and exams in Equality & Diversity, to challenge all forms of prejudice, starting from Year 1 and continuing every school year. Production of the exam results should be compulsory for all job applications. This would, over time, debunk and diminish bigoted ideas; creating understanding, respect and community cohesion, without the need for hate speech legislation.

People aren't born hateful. They become hateful. Education can prevent hate. Prevention is better than punishment.

13

Free Speech Is Essential on College Campuses

Greg Lukianoff

Greg Lukianoff is an attorney, as well as president and CEO of the Foundation for Individual Rights in Education (FIRE). He has also authored books about campus censorship and freedom from speech and co-authored a guide to free speech on campus.

The Donald Trump campaign and his subsequent presidency stirred the emotions of many college students to a greater extent than at any time since the Vietnam War. Scheduled speakers defending right-wing causes were sometimes booed to the point of being unable to properly deliver their messages or prevented from speaking altogether. In the following viewpoint, Lukianoff derides, through his organization, those who he perceives to be forcing censorship on college campuses and restricting the American ideals of freedom of speech.

2 015 will be remembered as a year in which campus free speech issues took center stage, receiving extensive coverage in outlets like *The New York Times*, *Wall Street Journal*, *The Atlantic*, *Slate*, *Vox*, and *Salon*. Even President Obama voiced concerns about the lack of debate on college campuses.

For those of us who have been fighting campus censors for years, it's hard not to ask: "Where has everyone been?"

"Campus Free Speech Has Been in Trouble for a Long Time," by Greg Lukianoff, Cato Unbound, January 4, 2016. Reprinted by permission.

My organization, the Foundation for Individual Rights in Education (FIRE), has been defending freedom of expression on campus since 1999. We can attest that free speech, open inquiry, and academic freedom have always been threatened on campus by one force or another, even long before we were founded.

Most people are familiar with the supposed heyday of political correctness of the 1980s and 90s, but there is a popular misconception that speech codes and censorship were defeated in the courts of law and public opinion by the mid-90s. In reality, the threats to campus speech never went away. Before examining what has changed to alarm the public—rightfully—about the state of open discourse in higher education, it's important to note what hasn't changed.

Speech Codes and Political Correctness Never Went Away

Scholars, including First Amendment expert Robert O'Neil, claim that politically correct speech codes were given a "decent burial" in the mid-90s. But despite being repeatedly defeated in court, speech codes became the rule rather than the exception on campus.

FIRE has been tracking and rating speech codes at hundreds of colleges and universities since 2006. Eight years ago, 75 percent of the institutions we surveyed maintained policies worthy of FIRE's "red light" rating, meaning they clearly and substantially restricted freedom of speech. Since then, the percentage of schools with red light speech codes has steadily declined each year.

This good news is due, at least in part, to FIRE's aggressive campaigning and lawsuits. Over the past few years, the number of campuses with red light policies decreased from 62.1 percent (2013) to 55.2 percent (2015). And, in FIRE's 2016 speech code report, that figure is below 50 percent (49.3 percent) for the first time. Unfortunately, this may be only a temporary high-water mark; pressure from students and the federal government makes the resurgence of speech codes almost inevitable.

The past 15 years are rife with examples of speech-policing. There are the classic political correctness cases, such as the 2004 incident in which a University of New Hampshire student was evicted from his dorm for posting flyers joking that freshman women could lose the "Freshman 15" by walking up the dormitory stairs. In 2009, Yale University students were told they shouldn't quote F. Scott Fitzgerald, and Bucknell University students were forbidden from handing out "Obama Stimulus Dollars."

But many cases do not follow the "PC" mold and just involve old-fashioned abuses of power. Examples include the University of Wisconsin-Stout's censorship of a professor's "Firefly" poster, Central New Mexico Community College's shutdown of a student newspaper for publishing a "Sex Issue," and former Valdosta State University student Hayden Barnes' unjust expulsion for protesting a parking garage (which led to an eight-year-long legal battle that finally concluded in 2015).

Federal Antidiscrimination Law as the Secret Engine of Campus Censorship

Some trends that long precede (and may explain) the current threats to campus free speech include the massive expansion of the bureaucratic class at universities, which officially began outnumbering the number of full-time instructors in 2005, and the rise of the "risk management" industry, which makes a fortune teaching universities how to avoid lawsuits by regulating almost every aspect of student life.

This brings us to the institution that is perhaps most responsible for exacerbating the problems of speech codes and hair-trigger censorship: the Department of Education's Office for Civil Rights (OCR).

By the late 1980s, colleges were adopting "anti-harassment" codes that restricted protected speech. In the mid-1990s, the campus speech code phenomenon converged with the expansion of federal anti-discrimination law by the Department of Education's Office for Civil Rights (OCR). OCR encouraged and even required harassment codes, and although its guidance tried to "balance" the need for these codes with the First Amendment, by the time FIRE was founded in 1999, universities were using the "federal government made me do it" excuse to justify even the most laughably unconstitutional speech codes.

In 2003, in perhaps its most redeeming moment, OCR issued a letter clarifying that it has no power to mandate that universities—public or private—police speech that is protected under the First Amendment. OCR explained that public universities, which are bound by the First Amendment, cannot ban merely offensive speech. And if private universities, which are not bound by the First Amendment (except in California through the Leonard Law), pass such speech codes, OCR made clear that they can in no way argue that the federal government forced their hand.

This message was never fully accepted by campus administrators, who wanted expansive speech codes, or by risk managers, who believed it was safer to discourage offensive speech than face a lawsuit. Nonetheless, the 2003 letter did help defuse an old excuse.

Unfortunately, the Department of Education under the Obama administration has been much more aggressive, granting itself new powers and redefining harassment in such broad language that virtually any offensive speech could be considered a matter of federal oversight.

In May 2013, OCR and the Department of Justice (DOJ) entered into a resolution agreement with the University of Montana that the agencies deemed "a blueprint for colleges and universities throughout the country." This "blueprint" mandates an extraordinarily broad definition of sexual harassment: "any unwelcome conduct of a sexual nature," including "verbal conduct"—i.e., speech. The blueprint holds that this conduct need not be "objectively offensive" to constitute sexual harassment. This means that if a listener takes offense to any sex- or gender-related speech, no matter how irrationally or unreasonably, the speaker has engaged in sexual harassment. Additionally, the final UM policy reviewed and approved by OCR and DOJ as part of their resolution agreement goes beyond policing sex-related speech by also prohibiting discriminatory harassment on the basis of 17 different categories, including "political ideas."

Treating this resolution agreement as a "blueprint" puts public universities in an impossible situation: violate the First Amendment or risk investigation and the possible loss of federal funding.

OCR backed away from its characterization of the Montana agreement as a "blueprint" in a November 2013 letter to me. But unlike the clarification it issued in 2003, OCR has never communicated this to universities. As a result, as universities revise their sexual misconduct policies, they now include the blueprint's definition of sexual harassment. There can be little doubt that the number of institutions doing so will only increase until OCR clarifies that it cannot require universities to adopt such a definition.

OCR is unlikely to forego unconstitutional speech-policing any time soon. In October, OCR announced that it would open a Title IX investigation into the University of Mary Washington after students filed a complaint about the school's handling of sexist and racist Yik Yak posts. If this investigation leads to new federal "guidance" on colleges' responsibility to police students' social media activity, even more protected campus speech could be threatened.

What Has Changed: Students Using Their Free Speech to Limit Free Speech

The biggest and most noticeable change in campus censorship in recent years has been the shift in student attitudes. Today, students often demand freedom from speech rather than freedom of speech.

Media coverage of the campus free speech crisis exploded in 2014 after a rash of "disinvitations"—student and faculty attempts to disinvite controversial speakers from campus, including former Secretary of State Condoleezza Rice and International Monetary Fund head Christine Lagarde.

Attention from the media has increased as more student-led efforts have gained popularity, such as demands for "trigger warnings" and "safe spaces," and efforts to police so-called "microaggressions." Critiquing PC culture is nothing new for conservative outlets, but even left-leaning authors at the New Republic, The Nation, New York Magazine, and The New York Times have been writing extensively about how these trends reflect very new, often alarming student attitudes about open discourse.

In my 15 years at FIRE, students have historically been the most reliably pro-free-speech constituency on campus. Students often showed more common sense than the professoriate, and certainly much more than the administrators.

But when stories about campus race-related protests inundated the news in the fall of 2015, I knew something had changed. It began when students at Wesleyan University demanded that the school's primary student newspaper be defunded after it published a student op-ed that was critical of the Black Lives Matter movement. Shortly after, Wesleyan's student government unanimously approved a resolution that will tentatively cut the paper's printing budget by half.

Things escalated when I saw firsthand that Yale students were demanding the resignations of two faculty members for sending out an email that questioned whether universities should tell students what they should or shouldn't wear as Halloween costumes. Then, just days later, student protests at the University of Missouri soured when protesters manhandled a student journalist.

These protests put First Amendment defenders and free speech advocates like me in a somewhat difficult position. Of course, I'm supportive of students exercising their free speech rights. Indeed, I find it refreshing that students have overcome their oft-diagnosed apathy towards serious social issues. However, it's distressing that many of the protesters are using their free speech to demand limitations on others' free speech. The irony of these demands was particularly prominent at the University of Missouri, where FIRE recently helped pass a state law making it illegal to limit free speech activities on public university campuses to tiny zones. This new law helped make the Mizzou students' protests possible. But in a twist, the protesters created their own free speech exclusion zone to prevent media from covering the protest.

Now student protestors at at least 75 American colleges and universities have released lists of demands "to end systemic and structural racism on campus." Although this is a laudable goal, a troubling number of these demands would prohibit or chill campus speech.

For example, many of the demands try to make the expression of racial bias, which is generally protected speech, a punishable offense. At Johns Hopkins University, protesters demand "impactful repercussions" for anyone who makes "Black students uncomfortable or unsafe for racial reasons." Similarly, protesters at Georgia's Kennesaw State University demand "strong repercussions and sanctions" for those who commit "racist actions and racial bias on campus." And Emory University protestors want a bias response reporting system and sanctions for even "unintentional" acts or behaviors, including "gestures."

Others go as far as to mandate that universities forbid "hate speech." At Missouri State University, protesters demand that administrators announce a "commitment to differentiating 'hate speech' from 'freedom of speech.'" Protesters at Dartmouth College want "a policy with serious consequences against hate speech/crimes (e.g. Greek house expelled for racist parties)." Similarly, student protesters at the University of Wyoming demand that the code of conduct be revised to hold students accountable for hate speech, complete with "a detailed reporting structure."

The evidence that today's students value freedom of speech less than their elders is not just anecdotal. In October, Yale University's William F. Buckley, Jr. Program released a survey that found that 51 percent of U.S. college students favor campus speech codes, and that 72 percent support disciplinary action against "any student or faculty member on campus who uses language that is considered racist, sexist, homophobic or otherwise offensive." These troubling results were echoed by a November 2015 global survey from Pew Research Center finding that a whopping 40 percent of U.S. millennials [ages 18–34] believe the government should be able to punish speech offensive to minority groups (as compared to only 12 percent of the Silent generation [70–87 year-olds], 24 percent of the Boomer generation [51–69 year-olds], and 27 percent of Gen Xers [35–50 year-olds]).

Conclusion

Thankfully, through old strategies and new ones, we can improve the climate for free speech on campus. Just one student or professor can protect free expression for thousands, or even hundreds of thousands, by filing a lawsuit against his or her school with the help of FIRE's Stand Up For Speech Litigation Project. SUFS is undefeated so far and has resulted in seven settlements that send the clear message to institutions that it will be expensive to ignore their obligations under the First Amendment. What's more, with every speech-protective judgment, it becomes harder for administrators to defend themselves with "qualified immunity," which shields individuals from personal liability where the law isn't clear.

Litigation might also be our best shot at forcing OCR to step back from its efforts to coerce institutions into adopting unconstitutional policies. Clearer and narrower policies than OCR's May 2013 definition of "sexual harassment" have been struck down in court on numerous occasions. But until institutions see a real threat of an expensive judgment against them for overbroad harassment policies, they'll continue to be motivated by the threat of OCR pulling their funding for what it seems to consider underbroad policies—i.e., colleges will err on the side of prohibiting protected expression.

And because money talks, alumni should withhold donations to institutions that break the law or renege on promises to respect students' and professors' rights. And of course, anyone can contact his or her legislators and ask them to support bills—like the ones FIRE helped enact in Missouri and Virginia—that ensure students may fully exercise their free speech rights on public campuses statewide.

These strategies may motivate schools to make quick changes, but free speech advocates know that long-lasting progress comes through cultural change. How do we teach a generation about the value of free expression when speech is too often presented as a problem to be overcome, rather than part of the solution to many social ills? This is our great challenge, and it must be faced with both determination and creativity if the always-fragile right of freedom of speech is to endure.

14

In Defense of "Uncomfortable Learning"

Alex Morey and Adam Steinbaugh

Alex Morey holds a law degree as well as a master of science in broadcast journalism. Adam Steinbaugh is an attorney who writes about free speech, the First Amendment, and the Internet. The Foundation for Individual Rights in Education (FIRE) works to defend and sustain its principles in American colleges and universities, including the right to freedom of speech. Among its core missions is to educate the public about the threats to such rights on campuses and seeking to preserve them.

In this article, the two authors lambast a threat of hate speech that motivated Williams College to ban a controversial speaker from presenting on campus. Alex Morey and Adam Steinbaugh detail the events leading up to the "disinviting" of a guest asked to campus by a student group for the very purpose of "uncomfortable learning." The authors believe that it is in the best interest of students to be exposed to all sides of an issue no matter how distasteful one viewpoint might be.

Williams College has disinvited a second speaker from its student-run "Uncomfortable Learning" speaker series, a program specifically developed to bring controversial viewpoints to campus. Unlike the first disinvitation, which came at the behest

"Williams College Bars 'Uncomfortable Learning' Speaker from Campus, Declares 'Hate Speech' Too Uncomfortable," by Alex Morey and Adam Steinbaugh, Foundation for Individual Rights in Education, February 18, 2016. Reprinted by permission.

of the speaker series' student organizers, this order came directly from the college president.

Williams President Adam Falk said in a statement to the university community this morning that he was canceling next Monday's speech by writer John Derbyshire, whose views have previously been called racist and sexist.

Falk blamed "hate speech" for the disinvitation:

To the Williams Community,

Today I am taking the extraordinary step of canceling a speech by John Derbyshire, who was to have presented his views here on Monday night. The college didn't invite Derbyshire, but I have made it clear to the students who did that the college will not provide a platform for him.

Free speech is a value I hold in extremely high regard. The college has a very long history of encouraging the expression of a range of viewpoints and giving voice to widely differing opinions. We have said we wouldn't cancel speakers or prevent the expression of views except in the most extreme circumstances. In other words: There's a line somewhere, but in our history of hosting events and speeches of all kinds, we hadn't yet found it.

We've found the line. Derbyshire, in my opinion, is on the other side of it. Many of his expressions clearly constitute hate speech, and we will not promote such speech on this campus or in our community.

We respect—and expect—our students' exploration of ideas, including ones that are very challenging, and we encourage individual choice and decision-making by students. But at times it's our role as educators and administrators to step in and make decisions that are in the best interest of students and our community. This is one of those times.

Sincerely,

Adam Falk

President

This isn't the first time Uncomfortable Learning has rendered the Williams community, well, uncomfortable.

Williams made headlines last October when student protests prompted Uncomfortable Learning to rescind its invitation to self-described "cultural critic" Suzanne Venker. As FIRE reported at the time, the college itself was not involved in Venker's disinvitation.

The college describes the Uncomfortable Learning program as follows:

> Uncomfortable Learning is a student-run, alumni-funded organization that aims to encourage students to understand and engage with often provocative and uncomfortable viewpoints that oppose perceived popular opinions at the College.
>
> […]
>
> "The goal of uncomfortable learning," said [a student organizer], "is to understand how someone who is just as sure as you are in their beliefs can think something completely different," but he added that the express purpose of the organization is not to convince people to change their beliefs.

Williams confirmed this morning that Uncomfortable Learning had indeed been the ones to invite Derbyshire:

> **Williams College** @WilliamsCollege 17 Feb
> @aarcher510 The college is not paying the speaker. UL's funding does not come from the college.

> **Veronica Hudson** @luther_swag
> @WilliamsCollege have you decided to actually take a stance on the White Supremacist speaker UL is bringing to campus?#SpeakOutPlease
> 7:31 AM - 18 Feb 2016

While student organizers canceled Suzanne Venker's October speech following student criticism, this cancellation was by the president of Williams College—the same president who, just last October, spoke convincingly and unreservedly about his commitment to respecting students' rights to bring controversial speakers to campus:

> When a controversial speaker – whose views on feminism I object to profoundly, by the way – was first invited and then

uninvited to speak, we drew a torrent of public criticism for what was perceived widely as an unwillingness of our community to tolerate the expression of differing viewpoints.

Let me be absolutely clear: Williams has a long history of inviting controversial speakers to campus and no history of uninviting them, and this is a point of absolute principle. Ours is an institution of higher learning; such learning cannot occur without broad and enthusiastic exposure to a wide range of ideas and perspectives. And certainly the invitation of a speaker to campus isn't in and of itself an endorsement – by the College or by individuals who invite a speaker – of that person's views. Whatever our own views may be, we should be active in bringing to campus speakers whose opinions are different from our own.

There is no reconciling Falk's October position with his current one, leaving students with unclear guidelines as to which speakers or subjects are out-of-bounds at Williams College. In fact, the only thing that is clear now is that President Falk has declared his administration to be the sole arbiter of what can and cannot be said at the college, the college's supposed commitment to free speech notwithstanding.

Although Williams is, as a private institution, free to craft its own rules, it has stated that it is "committed to being a community in which all ranges of opinion and belief can be expressed and debated" and that "controversy is at the heart of … free academic inquiry." Imposing restrictions on what topics may be discussed and who students may invite to discuss them is the polar opposite of "free academic inquiry"; it is closer to indoctrination than education.

FIRE keeps a comprehensive database of disinvitation incidents on campuses around the country.

It's worth noting that some of the most controversial speakers invited to speak at colleges and universities over the past century have sparked the adoption of policies that protect robust and open debate on campuses. The prime example is Yale's 1975 Woodward Report, which is regarded as the first free speech policy statement by a university to espouse a deep commitment to examining all viewpoints, no matter their popularity, as a path toward truth. That report was adopted only after students called for the disinvitation of controversial Nobel laureate William Shockley, whose views many contended were not only patently racist, but incontrovertibly false. The Woodward Report has been cited as an inspiration for the University of Chicago's free speech policy statement, which FIRE has endorsed, and which schools are increasingly adopting.

For the moment, it appears Williams has chosen a different path—a path on which paternalistic administrators decide which ideas are too dangerous for college students to hear, even when students themselves have established a program specifically for the purpose of engaging with such ideas. It is now up to the students, faculty, alumni, and trustees of Williams to decide whether that is truly the kind of place they want their college to be, or whether they are going to push back against this act of censorship.

15

Censoring Hate Speech Makes Sense

Sean McElwee

Sean McElwee is a policy analyst at Demos, a public policy organization. He has written essays for The Atlantic, The New Republic, Rolling Stone, The Washington Post, and Politico, among other publications.

In modern, technology-fueled times, hate speech is not solely expressed through spoken word. In this essay, McElwee discusses occurrences of hate speech on social media sites such as Facebook and Twitter, some of which have spurred discourse on the thorny issue of censorship. McElwee places himself firmly on the side of taking stronger steps to prevent those who spew hate from having a voice. He cites European models that have gained success silencing those he perceives as harmful to society.

For the past few years, speech has moved online, leading to fierce debates about its regulation. Most recently, feminists have led the charge to purge Facebook of misogyny that clearly violates its hate speech code. Facebook took a small step two weeks ago, creating a feature that will remove ads from pages deemed "controversial." But such a move is half-hearted; Facebook and other social networking websites should not tolerate hate speech and, in the absence of a government mandate, adopt a European model of expunging offensive material.

"Human Rights: The Case for Censoring Hate Speech," by Sean McElwee, Alternet / Alternet.org, July 12, 2013. Reprinted by permission.

Stricter regulation of Internet speech will not be popular with the libertarian-minded citizens of the United States, but it's necessary. A typical view of such censorship comes from Jeffrey Rosen, who argues in The New Republic that,

> ...given their tremendous size and importance as platforms for free speech, companies like Facebook, Google, Yahoo, and Twitter shouldn't try to be guardians of what Waldron calls a "well-ordered society"; instead, they should consider themselves the modern version of Oliver Wendell Holmes's fractious marketplace of ideas—democratic spaces where all values, including civility norms, are always open for debate.

This image is romantic and lovely (although misattributed to Oliver Wendell Holmes, who famously toed both lines on the free speech debate, instead of John Stuart Mill) but it's worth asking what this actually looks like. Rosen forwards one example:

> Last year, after the French government objected to the hash tag "#unbonjuif"—intended to inspire hateful riffs on the theme "a good Jew ..."—Twitter blocked a handful of the resulting tweets in France, but only because they violated French law. Within days, the bulk of the tweets carrying the hashtag had turned from anti-Semitic to denunciations of anti-Semitism, confirming that the Twittersphere is perfectly capable of dealing with hate speech on its own, without heavy-handed intervention.

It's interesting to note how closely this idea resembles free market fundamentalism: simply get rid of any coercive rules and the "marketplace of ideas" will naturally produce the best result. Humboldt State University compiled a visual map that charts150,000 hateful insults aggregated over the course of 11 months in the U.S. by pairing Google's Maps API with a series of the most homophobic, racist and otherwise prejudiced tweets. The map's existence draws into question the notion that the "twittersphere" can organically combat hate speech; hate speech is not going to disappear from twitter on its own.

The negative impacts of hate speech do not lie in the responses of third-party observers, as hate speech aims at two goals. First, it is an attempt to tell bigots that they are not alone. Frank Collins —the neo-Nazi prosecuted in *National Socialist Party of America v Skokie* (1977) — said, "We want to reach the good people, get the fierce anti-Semites who have to live among the Jews to come out of the woodwork and stand up for themselves."

The second purpose of hate speech is to intimidate the targeted minority, leading them to question whether their dignity and social status is secure. In many cases, such intimidation is successful. Consider the number of rapes that go unreported. Could this trend possibly be impacted by Reddit threads like /r/rapingwomen or /r/mensrights? Could it be due to the harassment women face when they even suggest the possibility they were raped? The rape culture that permeates Facebook, Twitter and the public dialogue must be held at least partially responsible for our larger rape culture.

Reddit, for instance, has become a veritable potpourri of hate speech; consider Reddit threads like /r/nazi, /r/killawoman, /r/misogny, /r/killingwomen. My argument is not that these should be taken down because they are offensive, but rather because they amount to the degradation of a class that has been historically oppressed. Imagine a Reddit thread for /r/lynchingblacks or /r/assassinatingthepresident. We would not argue that we should sit back and wait for this kind of speech be "outspoken" by positive speech, but that it should be entirely banned.

American free speech jurisprudence relies upon the assumption that speech is merely the extension of a thought, and not an action. If we consider it an action, then saying that we should combat hate speech with more positive speech is an absurd proposition; the speech has already done the harm, and no amount of support will defray the victim's impression that they are not truly secure in this society. We don't simply tell the victim of a robbery, "Hey, it's okay, there are lots of other people who aren't going to rob you." Similarly, it isn't incredibly useful to tell someone who has just had their race/gender/sexuality defamed, "There are a lot of other nice people out there."

Those who claim to "defend free speech" when they defend the right to post hate speech online, are in truth backwards. Free speech isn't an absolute right; no right is weighed in a vacuum. The court has imposed numerous restrictions on speech. Fighting words, libel and child pornography are all banned. Other countries merely go one step further by banning speech intended to intimidate vulnerable groups. The truth is that such speech does not democratize speech, it monopolizes speech. Women, LGBTQ individuals and racial or religious minorities feel intimidated and are left out of the public sphere. On Reddit, for example, women have left or changed their usernames to be more male-sounding lest they face harassment and intimidation for speaking on Reddit about even the most gender-neutral topics.

Those who try to remove this hate speech have been criticized from left and right. At Slate, Jillian York writes, "While the campaigners on this issue are to be commended for raising awareness of such awful speech on Facebook's platform, their proposed solution is ultimately futile and sets a dangerous precedent for special interest groups looking to bring their pet issue to the attention of Facebook's censors."

It hardly seems right to qualify a group fighting hate speech as an "interest group" trying to bring their "pet issue" to the attention of Facebook censors. The "special interest" groups she fears might apply for protection must meet Facebook's strict community standards, which state:

> While we encourage you to challenge ideas, institutions, events, and practices, we do not permit individuals or groups to attack others based on their race, ethnicity, national origin, religion, sex, gender, sexual orientation, disability or medical condition.

If anything, the groups to which York refers are nudging Facebook towards actually enforcing its own rules.

People who argue against such rules generally portray their opponents as standing on a slippery precipice, tugging at the question "what next?" We can answer that question: Canada, England, France, Germany, The Netherlands, South Africa,

Australia and India all ban hate speech. Yet, none of these countries have slipped into totalitarianism. In many ways, such countries are more free when you weigh the negative liberty to express harmful thoughts against the positive liberty that is suppressed when you allow for the intimidation of minorities.

As Arthur Schopenhauer said, "the freedom of the press should be governed by a very strict prohibition of all and every anonymity." However, with the Internet the public dialogue has moved online, where hate speech is easy and anonymous.

Jeffrey Rosen argues that norms of civility should be open to discussion, but, in today's reality, this issue has already been decided; impugning someone because of their race, gender or orientation is not acceptable in a civil society. Banning hate speech is not a mechanism to further this debate because the debate is over.

As Jeremy Waldron argues, hate speech laws prevent bigots from, "trying to create the impression that the equal position of members of vulnerable minorities in a rights-respecting society is less secure than implied by the society's actual foundational commitments."

Some people argue that the purpose of laws that ban hate speech is merely to avoid offending prudes. No country, however, has mandated that anything be excised from the public square merely because it provokes offense, but rather because it attacks the dignity of a group—a practice the U.S. Supreme Court called in Beauharnais v. Illinois (1952) "group libel." Such a standard could easily be applied to Twitter, Reddit and other social media websites. While Facebook's policy as written should be a model, it's enforcement has been shoddy. Chaim Potok argues that if a company claims to have a policy, it should rigorously and fairly enforce it.

If this is the standard, the Internet will surely remain controversial, but it can also be free of hate and allow everyone to participate. A true marketplace of ideas must co-exist with a multi-racial, multi-gender, multi-sexually-oriented society, and it can.

16

Hatred for Hate Speech Is Misplaced

BlackCatte

BlackCatte is a regular contributor to OffGuardian, a website that touts itself as an alternative to mainstream media. It sees itself as expressing the truth and embracing the sanctity of truth.

Are free speech and hate speech really about power? In the following viewpoint, the author suggests that the motivation to limit hate speech on the Internet is not to curb racism, sexism or anti-gay sentiment, but rather to kill freedom of speech by allowing those in power to become the equivalent of thought police. The author further contends that greed, power, and paranoia are behind the push to censor hate speech on the Internet, but only through persuading ordinary people of its merits can that push succeed.

T he current – and frankly bizarre even by recent standards – Guardian campaign "the web we want" seems to be driven by two main agendas. The first, and probably the major one is the long-simmering plan to "regulate" (i.e. control and censor) free speech on the Web. That the Graun's effort is part of a coordinated new offensive in that department is pretty conclusively illustrated by the fact the ex-minister for "equality", Maria Miller delivered her own diatribe against the "problem" of internet "abuse" just days after the Guardian's new campaign took off. The similarity between her invective and that employed by the Guardian's tame

"End Free Speech and Save the Minorities! (Will Anyone Really Fall for This?)," by BlackCatte, OffGuardian, April 14, 2016. Reprinted by permission.

journos puts it beyond question that this is an Establishment-wide move. A concerted plan to use exaggerated claims of "abuse" and its alleged impact on minorities, to mobilise well-meaning liberals in support of internet censorship.

In fact, unlike the feeble Apologists at Graun HQ, Miller at least has the guts to pretty much say so out loud:

> We need better laws and we need better enforcement. Government needs to stop allowing internet providers from(sic) hiding behind arguments about the protection of free speech.

Right there we have it. The plan they formulated in their focus groups and policy committees. The best way to get the internet censorship they have wanted for so long is to pretend it isn't censorship at all, but protection! And most particularly protection of those sections of society we all know need it most. The ethnic minorities, the LGBT communities – and women. The mere mention of these groups will be enough to rally many well-meaning but naive liberals to support their own gagging. "I'm happy to have my right to anonymity abolished if it helps stamp out racial abuse" they'll say. "I'm happy to see comments sections closed if it helps women columnists avoid harassment", they'll say. There'll probably be a social media campaign with a catchy soundbite and the same soft focus unthreatening images of "diversity" they pull up at the Graun. And people will sign up to be silenced.

But of course it won't end racism or sexism or homophobia. Because it's not intended to. The people behind this couldn't give a flying feck for the wellbeing of minorities or anyone else beyond their own narrow class of super-privilege. That's just window dressing. A lure for the gullible. It's the Child Catcher prancing about in borrowed gaudy, his cage draped in pictures of candy.

The truth is they want to kill the internet and all its unparalleled power to monitor them and their variously greedy, stupid, paranoid antics. And they know they can't do that unless they can persuade most ordinary people it's a good idea.

This is why over the coming weeks and months you'll see Owen Jones and other unscrupulous hacks (yes, we're sorry, but Jones deserves no better descriptor after his recent ghastly display), trying to repackage free speech as "elitist" and using tortured pseudo-logic to "prove" that censorship is the only way to have truly open debate.

The second part of the Guardian agenda is to try to roll back the massive damage being done to its reputation by the current CiF debacle.

Since its inception in 2006, CiF ("Comment is Free") was hailed as the Guardian's flagship of credibility, their pledge of openness and inclusiveness. And for a while it was. Most stories were open for discussion. Moderation was decorous. If it was politically motivated sometimes, it was discreet enough to have only minimal impact (mostly on stories about Israel). By and large CiF at that time was a real place for the sharing of information and opinion. All was reasonably well.

But somewhere around 2012-13 things began to change. Did the Government losing the Syria vote and the widespread opposition to a war against Assad signal to the PTB that open discussion of vital news stories was beginning to have unexpected consequences for their control of the narrative? Did the Snowden issue persuade people they'd rather get inline than risk their pension plans?

In any event moderation became more insistent. Not – whatever the official line may be – because the trolls were more prolific or persistent. They weren't. Trolls are to the internet what rats are to cities. They are always there, but their impact on most of us is minimal. Civilised discussion proceeds above and around them. Trolls are trolls and never really change. No, what changed was that for maybe the first time there was a noticeable tendency to censor for opinion. Not racist opinion, or sexist opinion. Just anti-government opinion. Or minority opinion. At first it was relatively minor. – But then in February 2014 the West decided to go insane and provoke WW3 in Ukraine and everything changed forever.

News outlets like the Guardian and the BBC stood by and vaguely cheered this act of insanity, as if too lobotomised to even understand what was going on. We saw Shaun Walker making facile jokes about vodka and potatoes. Luke Harding, off his meds and off his leash squealing Russophobic paranoia. We saw crazed old NATO generals foaming at the mouth for war, and slick intelligence types citing reams of easily disproven statistics to "prove" Russia was the problem. What we didn't see – anywhere – in the Establishment media was any voice of sanity, warning that this was a new Cuban Missile crisis and that more was required of us than xenophobia and soundbites.

The CiF sections – naturally – erupted in shock and incredulity that the Guardian – the Guardian – could possibly be fielding such stupid, dangerous, and low-grade propaganda. The comments were something like 10-1, if not more, in opposition to the hardline editorial stance and pleading for some realisation of what madness our governments were engaged in. And that's when the Great Cull began.

As the official Western narrative on Ukraine unraveled in the face of the Odessa massacre, the black farce of the ATO and multiple revelations of how close the new government's ties to neo-nazis really were, so the Guardian's own line became increasingly nakedly propagandist. It set up a network with publications such as the Kiev Post and Radio Free Europe, and disseminated their dishonest hit pieces and fake propaganda stories without question or demur. In a matter of months it had become unrecognisable to those who had formerly respected it. Either it fundamentally changed at this time, or, maybe more likely, it simply stopped pretending. Either way, it stopped being the Guardian in any sense that meant anything.

At the same time moderation in CiF became for the first time overtly politicised, if not draconian. As people reacted more and more to the changing tone ATL, so more and more censorship was required BTL to keep that reaction in check. Comments that asserted a Russian perspective, or that simply called for some sort of middle ground were many times more likely to be blocked than those that supported the NATO position. Extreme racism toward

Russians became more and more acceptable both ATL and BTL, while even minor critique of the Guardian's own authors became punishable by not just blocking but outright banning.

But even the most intense efforts to control the debate proved futile. Whenever they opened a story for comments on Ukraine, Syria, or any other NATO war zone, it would be flooded with people opposing the warmongering of our governments, or questioning the veracity of the article, or linking to different versions of the story or to other stories the Guardian was choosing not to run. Try as they might to take down links, block comments, ban accounts, they couldn't stop this tide.

And worse, people were now commenting on the censorship of comments, requiring even more censorship in turn. They developed zero tolerance for anyone questioning why a given comment had been taken down. if you dared ask why you were blocked or banned. They began pre-emptively banning certain accounts for a given period when sensitive news stories were broken, un-blocking them again after a decent interval. They seem to have added certain websites (including this one) to lists of URLS that would be immediately removed whatever content they contained.

But the more they censored, the more they were called on for their censorship, and the harder it became to pretend – even to themselves – that they were still the lovely liberal Guardian embracing free speech. They might tell each other they were censoring "trolls" or "Putinbots", but in their hearts they knew, and knew that their readers all knew, what was really going on.

CiF is now one of their major problems. They need to preserve it – their once proud flagship – in order to cling to the remnants of their self-image as leaders of free thought. They can rename it "Opinion", as if that makes the absence of Free Comment somehow less real. They can censor it to the point of destruction. But they can't close it down. Because that would be admitting what they are and admitting defeat.

"The web we want" is their own, strangely pathetic, attempt at squaring that circle. You can look at it almost like the inner dialogue of a deeply troubled psyche. Self-soothing with repetition and over-assertion.

Those bizarre and strained attempts at "explaining" their comment policy with graphs and "research" so openly bogus it proves nothing beyond their own desperation. Those weird photoshoots of confused but smiling "Best CiF Commenters" (chosen by "cross-referencing a list of the commenters who had the highest average of "recommends per comment" with a list of those with the highest percentage of "staff picks"), designed to show how comfortable they really are with their own readership, but being about as convincing as a kidnap victim reading a scrawled note to camera about how well he is being treated.

Hysterical. Hopeless. And deeply sad. Because even if this new agenda of cuddly censorship to help minorities does get enough of a claw hold to make a difference, and even if we all do lose our remaining freedoms, the Guardian is dead to most of its old readers. Its moral base has been destroyed, its reputation is irreparably shredded. It's now just a glorified mag for clickbait and badly written agitprop. Its readership is shrinking, its income is vanishing. It's propped up now by its bosses in Washington and London, existing on their life support until it's been drained of all possible use, when they will turn off the machines and let it die.

The "journalists" who work for it won't much care when that happens of course. If they cared about such things they wouldn't be doing what they do. They'll just be paid off and move on to different positions, where they can enjoy expense account lunches and spurious feelings of security while it lasts. But many old readers will care quite a lot. Even though it will also feel like putting a suffering animal out of its misery.

17

Let's Make the Punishment Fit the Crime

Michael Lieberman

Michael Lieberman works as Washington counsel for the Anti-Defamation League. He has testified in support of hate crime laws to Congress and state legislatures. He has also schooled law enforcement officials in training centers throughout the United States and chaired a broad coalition of groups to improve the federal response to hate violence.

Michael Lieberman makes neither the argument for nor against banning or curbing hate speech. In the following viewpoint, he states simply that the First Amendment — as currently constituted — provides freedom of speech that includes hate speech. But he refutes the argument that hate crime laws will lead to the criminalization of hate speech and weaken the First Amendment. His assertion is that free speech protections indeed remain strong because of the First Amendment, and that the predictions of doom when hate crime laws were first established have never come to fruition.

Jesse Larner sounds a shrill alarm in his broadside against hate crime laws ("Hate Crime/Thought Crime," Spring 2010), raising a variety of seemingly dire libertarian, First Amendment, and slippery-slope arguments. Yet, despite the fact that federal and state hate crime laws have been on the books for forty years, he fails to illustrate his parade of horribles with a single actual case

"Hate Crime Laws: Punishment to Fit the Crime," by Michael Lieberman, Anti-Defamation League, July 8, 2010. Reprinted by permission.

to demonstrate the kind of "policing of mind and tongue" about which he frets.

Larner recognizes that hate crimes are a "real problem" and asks many of the right questions about the purpose and application of these laws. But Larner's questions have been thoroughly examined—and answered—by police officials and prosecutors who have enforced them and by dozens of court decisions interpreting these laws.

Larner is wrong about the impact of hate violence, the policy purposes of hate crime laws, and their constitutionality.

The Policy Rationale

The starting point is to recognize that criminal activity motivated by bias is different from other criminal conduct.

First, these crimes occur because of the perpetrator's bias or animus against the victim on the basis of actual or perceived status—the victim's race, religion, national origin, gender, gender identity, sexual orientation, or disability is the reason for the crime. In the vast majority of these crimes, absent the victim's personal characteristic, no crime would occur at all.

One recent, dramatic example of this phenomenon is the murder of Marcelo Lucero, a thirty-seven-year-old Ecuadoran immigrant who was killed in November 2008 in Patchogue, New York. According to the testimony of one of the Long Island teenagers who pleaded guilty to second-degree attempted assault as a hate crime, and other charges, several bored teenagers decided to go "beaner hopping"—a periodic practice in which they hunted Hispanics to beat up for sport. They had allegedly already shot at a Hispanic man on his porch with a BB gun and harassed another Hispanic man on a bike when they came across two Hispanic men near the Patchogue train station. The teenagers taunted the two with racist names and picked a fight. During the fight, Lucero was knifed. He subsequently died.

Second, hate violence is intentionally, specifically targeted at individuals because of their personal, immutable characteristics.

These are, therefore, very personal crimes, with very special emotional and psychological impact on the victim—and the victim's community. Hate crimes physically wound and may effectively intimidate other members of the victim's community, leaving them feeling terrorized, isolated, vulnerable, and unprotected by the law. By making the victim's community fearful, angry, and suspicious of other groups—and of the power structure that is supposed to protect them—these incidents can damage the fabric of our society and fragment communities. Larner cites House Judiciary Committee Chair John Conyers and former Human Rights Campaign senior counsel Cristina Finch for this proposition, but he is much too dismissive of its significance.

Hate crimes are message crimes. Gay men beaten outside of a gay bar are rarely robbed. Vandals do not often spray-paint messages like "Jane Loves Bobby" on the side of synagogues; it is much more frequently defacement featuring threats and a swastika. And bigots do not burn parallelograms on the front lawns of African American families who have just moved into a previously all-white neighborhood. The message of the parallelogram might be misunderstood. Not so the remains of a burned cross. As Supreme Court Justice Sandra Day O'Connor wrote in a 2003 case involving a First Amendment challenge to the Commonwealth of Virginia's cross-burning statute:

> … the burning cross often serves as a message of intimidation, designed to inspire in the victim a fear of bodily harm. Moreover, the history of violence associated with the Klan shows that the possibility of injury or death is not just hypothetical.…when a cross burning is used to intimidate, few if any messages are more powerful. (Virginia v. Black, 538U.S.343, 357 [2003])

In addition, over the past thirty years, many studies and surveys about hate violence—and the impact on the victims— indicate that these crimes are qualitatively different from other crimes. They are more serious ("…hate crimes are inherently more harmful to the social fabric than comparable crimes without bias motive," McDevitt, Balboni, Garcia, and Gu, 2001); more likely to involve violence ("…the victim of a hate crime assault is four times more likely to require hospital treatment than the victim of a parallel assault." McDevitt and Levin, 1993); more harmful in their aftermath ("The negative effects of hate crimes may be longer lasting than those of other crimes." Herek, Gillis, and Cogan, 1999).

Few individual crimes can spark riots, but bias-motivated crimes can. Civic leaders and police officials have come to recognize that strong enforcement of these laws can have a deterrent impact and can limit the potential for a hate crime incident to explode into a cycle of violence and widespread community disturbances.*

The FBI and law enforcement officials recognize the special impact of hate crimes. The FBI has been the nation's repository for crime statistics since 1930. It publishes an annual encyclopedic report called Crime in the United States. Every year, the FBI disaggregates that data and publishes two—only two—other separate reports on crime issues that it believes have a dramatic impact on Americans. One report is focused on law enforcement officers killed in the line of duty and the other is about hate crimes in America. In 2008, 13,690 police agencies reported 7,783 hate crimes—almost one hate crime for every hour of every day. Race-based hate crimes were most frequent, second were religion-based (anti-Jewish crimes composed a disturbing 66 percent of the reported religion crimes), and third most frequent were crimes against gay men and lesbians.

Larner seems to recognize the special nature of hate violence when he asserts that crimes in which the victim is intentionally selected for violence on the basis of racial bigotry can be rightly condemned as "morally worse" than other crimes. However, then he questions whether society can act to make them "legally worse."

We can and we should.

It was Sir William Blackstone, the eighteenth-century British legal scholar, who said that "it is but reasonable that among crimes of different natures those should be most severely punished, which are the most destructive of the public safety and happiness." In recognition of the odious nature of these crimes and their serious impact, it is entirely appropriate that they be treated differently.

We cannot outlaw hate, but laws shape attitudes. And attitudes influence behavior. We Americans have communally determined to try to prevent and remedy bigoted behavior in the housing market or workplace through thousands of federal, state, and local laws that prohibit invidious discrimination because of race or other identifying personal characteristics. In fact, hate crime laws are a criminal justice system parallel to these laws. In language, structure, and application, the majority of the nation's hate crime laws are directly analogous to anti-discrimination civil rights laws. Under our nation's workplace civil rights laws, for example, an employer can refuse to hire, fire, or fail to promote non-unionized employees for virtually any reason. It is only when that decision is made "by reason of" race, religion, national origin, gender, or disability (and in too-few state and local jurisdictions, sexual orientation) that the conduct becomes unlawful.

First Amendment Protections

Hate crime statutes—federal criminal civil rights statutes and laws now on the books in forty-five states and the District of Columbia—do not punish speech or thoughts. The First Amendment does not protect violence, nor does it prevent the government from imposing criminal penalties for violent discriminatory conduct directed against victims on the basis of their personal characteristics. Americans are free to think, preach, and believe whatever they want. It is only when an individual commits a crime based on those biased beliefs and intentionally targets another for violence or vandalism that a hate crime statute can be triggered.

Under these laws, a perpetrator can face more severe penalties only if the prosecutor can demonstrate, beyond a reasonable doubt, that the victim was intentionally targeted on the basis of his or her personal characteristics because of the perpetrator's bias against the victim.

Over the years, federal and state hate crime laws have been upheld against a variety of challenges under the Fourteenth Amendment's equal protection clause and due process clause, and under the First Amendment. The most important case, Wisconsin v. Mitchell, involved a challenge to Wisconsin's penalty-enhancement hate crime statute, under which Mitchell had received an enhanced sentence for having instigated a vicious racial assault by a group of young black men against a white boy in Kenosha, Wisconsin.

Larner wrongly claims that Mitchell was convicted "under a statute that criminalizes bigoted speech leading to violence." The Wisconsin hate crime law does no such thing. Instead, it provides enhanced sentencing when the perpetrator "intentionally selects the person against whom the crime [is committed] in whole or in part because of the actor's belief or perception regarding the race, religion, color, disability, sexual orientation, national origin or ancestry of that person…" Speech is not criminalized. The crime is triggered by conduct—when the perpetrator intentionally selects the victim for violence or vandalism because of the victim's personal characteristic.

The Supreme Court held that the Wisconsin statute was intended to address conduct that the Wisconsin legislature thought would "inflict greater individual and societal harm." Removing any doubt that such laws wrongly penalize speech, the Court held,

> The First Amendment … does not prohibit the evidentiary use of speech to establish the elements of a crime or to prove motive or intent. Evidence of a defendant's previous declarations or statements is commonly admitted in criminal trials subject to evidentiary rules dealing with relevancy, reliability, and the like. (Wisconsin v. Mitchell, 508 U.S. 476, 478 [1993])

The case attracted unusual attention. Among those who urged the Court to uphold the Wisconsin hate crime statute were many major law enforcement and civil rights organizations, including the National ACLU and the Anti-Defamation League (filing a brief for sixteen national civil rights and law enforcement organizations, including the unlikely pairing of the Fraternal Order of Police and the Center for Constitutional Rights) and a brief filed by the attorney general of Ohio on behalf of the other forty-nine states and the District of Columbia.

Larner plainly does not much like the Court's holding in Mitchell. He warns ominously about the First Amendment implications of the decision: "We are living with them now." But then: nothing! Eighteen years after the Supreme Court's decision, he fails to cite a single case to illustrate his dire concern—no misapplications of a statute, no overreach by a federal or state prosecutor, no sliding down a slippery slope.

Larner concludes with a final warning about the future: "[m]ake no mistake: hate crime laws do set us up for hate speech laws." He rightly notes that hate crime laws require an underlying crime—that speech or thought alone cannot create legal liability. But then he asserts that "it is but a small step" to criminalizing speech or thought alone. To illustrate his assertion, Larner detours northward across the border to Canada, where he grew up, to describe the experience Canada has had with criminalizing hate speech.

But the comparison fails. The United States is plainly not Canada—the First Amendment makes the United States unique. Many democratic countries penalize hate speech, and many criminalize Holocaust denial. That is not, however, the U.S. approach—and dire predictions that take into account neither the robust speech protections guaranteed by the First Amendment nor the forty-year experience with federal and state hate crime laws in this country fall flat.

On June 25, 2009, I testified before the Senate Judiciary Committee in support of the Matthew Shepard and James Byrd, Jr. Hate Crime Prevention Act on behalf of a broad coalition of civil rights, religious, education, civic, professional, and law enforcement organizations. I noted then that it was quite unusual for these groups to advocate for expanded federal police powers—and that it was even more extraordinary that we were doing so alongside virtually every major law enforcement organization in the country. This important legislation, signed into law by President Obama on October 28, 2009, provides important new tools to combat violent hate crimes and encourages federal-state partnerships to investigate and prosecute them.

We should have no delusions about hate crime laws. Bigotry, racism, homophobia, and anti-Semitism cannot be legislated out of existence. The law is absolutely a blunt instrument; it is much better to prevent these crimes from happening in the first place.

But when these crimes do occur, we must send an unmistakable message that they matter, that our society takes them very seriously. Hate crime laws demonstrate an important commitment to confront and deter criminal activity motivated by prejudice. Like anti-discrimination laws, hate crime statutes are content-neutral, color-blind mechanisms that appropriately allow society to redress a unique type of wrongful conduct in a manner that reflects that conduct's seriousness.

Hate violence merits priority attention—and hate crime laws help ensure they receive it.

Organizations to Contact

The editors have compiled the following list of organizations concerned with the issues debated in this book. The descriptions are derived from materials provided by the organizations. All have publications or information available for interested readers. The list was compiled on the date of publication of the present volume; the information provided here may change. Be aware that many organizations take several weeks or longer to respond to inquiries, so allow as much time as possible.

American Bar Association
1050 Connecticut Ave. NW, Washington, D.C. 20036.
(202) 662-1000
website: http://www.americanbar.org/aba

The American Bar Association is the center of legal profession in the United States. Its mission is not only to serve its members, but work toward the public good by defending liberty and delivering justice to all.

American Booksellers for Free Expression (ABFE)
333 Westchester Ave., Suite S202, White Plains, NY, 10604
(914) 406-7576
website: http://www.bookweb.org/abfe.

The mission of the American Booksellers for Free Expression is to promote and protect the free exchange of ideas, especially those in book form, by fighting against restrictions on the freedom of speech. The group also issues statements on free expression controversies, participates in legal cases involving First Amendment rights and works alongside other organizations with like-minded purposes.

American Civil Liberties Union (ACLU)
125 Broad St., 18th Floor, New York, N.Y. 10004
(212) 549-2500.
e-mail: https://www.aclu.org/contact-us
website: https://www.aclu.org/

The American Civil Liberties Union has for nearly a century worked to defend and preserve the individual rights and liberties guaranteed by the United States Constitution and laws of the nation. It has worked through the justice and political systems, as well as individual communities, to maintain the promise and application of liberty for all Americans.

American Library Association Office for Intellectual Freedom
50 E. Huron St., Chicago, IL 60611
(312) 280-4226
Website: http://www.ala.org/offices/oif

The Office for Intellectual Freedom works to implement policies created by the American Library Association. Among its goals is to educate the general public about the nature and importance of intellectual freedom and to support librarians, teachers, and administrators.

Anti-Defamation League
1736 Franklin St., 9th Floor
Oakland, CA 94612
(510) 208-7744
website: http://www.adl.org/

The Anti-Defamation League (ADL) was founded in 1913 to halt the defamation of Jewish people and secure justice and fair treatment for all Americans. It has since become one of the premier civil rights agency as it combats all forms of bigotry and promotes democratic ideals.

First Amendment Project
1736 Franklin St., 9th Floor, Oakland, CA 94612
(510) 208-7744
Fax: (510) 208-4562
website: https://www.thefirstamendment.org/

The First Amendment project works to uphold First Amendment rights for individuals and groups that cannot afford to gain legal representation. The organization specializes in helping journalists, documentarians, artists, activists, nonprofit organizations, and others who are sued for what they say or write.

Foundation for Individual Rights in Education (FIRE)
510 Walnut St., Suite 1250, Philadelphia, PA 19106
(215) 717-3473
Fax: (215) 717-3440
e-mail: fire@thefire.org
website: https://www.thefire.org/

FIRE seeks to defend and maintain individual rights on college campuses throughout the United States. Among those rights are freedom of speech, religious liberty, and legal equality.

National Coalition Against Censorship
19 Fulton St., Suite 407, New York, NY, 10038
(212) 807-6222
Fax: (212) 807-6245
e-mail: ncac@ncac.org
website: http://ncac.org

The stated mission of NCAC is to promote freedom of thought, inquiry, and expression, as well as to oppose censorship in all forms. It formed in response to a 1973 Supreme Court case that narrowed First Amendment protections.

Muslim Advocates
PO Box 71080, Oakland, CA, 94612
(415) 653-1897
website: https://www.muslimadvocates.org

This organization strives to guarantee freedom and justice for Americans of all faiths. It is a national legal advocacy and educational group.

PEN America
588 Broadway, Suite 303. New York, N.Y. 10012
(212) 334-1660
Fax: (212) 334-2181
email: info@pen.org
website: https://pen.org/

PEN America is a non-governmental organization affiliated with PEN International, a worldwide association of writers founded nearly a century ago to promote friendship and cooperation among writers everywhere while stressing the role of literature in developing an understanding. The group fights for freedom of expression and works on behalf of writers who have been harassed, jailed, or even murdered for their views.

Southern Poverty Law Center
400 Washington Ave., Birmingham, AL 36104
(888) 414-7752
website: https://www.splcenter.org/

The Southern Poverty Law Center is dedicated to fighting hate and bigotry while seeking justice for the most vulnerable people in American society. It uses the courts, education, and other forms of advocacy in working toward the ideals of equal justice and opportunity for all.

Student Press Law Center
1608 Rhode Island Ave. NW, Suite 211, Washington, DC 20036
(202) 785-5450
e-mail: splc@splc.org
website: http://www.splc.org/

The Student Press Law Center seeks to strike to protect the freedom to discuss issues of public concern. It audits the compliance of school districts with free-expression laws and publicize the results and offers tutorials for students who wish to advocate for freedom of expression.

Bibliography

Books

Thomas Garton Ash. *Free Speech: Ten Principles for a Connected World*. New Haven, CT: Yale University Press, 2016.

Eric Barendt: *Freedom of Speech*. New York, NY: Oxford University Press, 2007.

Robert L. Bernstein. *Speaking Freely: My Life in Publishing and Human Rights*. New York, NY: New Press, 2016.

Mary Katharine Ham and Guy Benson. *End of Discussion: How the Left's Outrage Industry Shuts Down Debate, and Makes America Less Free (and Fun)*. New York, NY: Crown Forum, 2015.

Ivan Hare and James Weinstein. *Extreme Speech and Democracy*. New York, NY: Oxford University Press, 2011.

Eric Heinze. *Hate Speech and Democratic Citizenship*. New York, NY: Oxford University Press, 2016.

Michael Herz and Peter Molnar, eds. *The Content and Context of Hate Speech*. New York, NY: Cambridge University Press, 2012.

Greg Lukianoff. *Unlearning Liberty: Campus Censorship and the End of American Debate*. New York, NY: Encounter Books, 2014.

Kirsten Powers: *The Silencing: How the Left is Killing Free Speech*. Washington, DC: Regnery Publishing, 2015.

Jonathan Rauch. *Kindly Inquisitors: The New Attacks on Free Thought*. Chicago, IL: University of Chicago Press, 2014.

David K. Shipler. *Freedom of Speech: Mightier Than the Sword*. New York, NY: Vintage Books, 2016.

Jeremy Waldron. *The Harm in Hate Speech (Oliver Wendell Holmes Lectures)*. Cambridge, MA: Harvard University Press, 2014.

Samuel Walker. *Hate Speech: The History of an American Controversy*. Lincoln, NE: University of Nebraska Press, 1994.

Periodicals and Internet Sources

Imtiaz Alam. "Hate speech is not free speech." *The International News*, February 9, 2017. https://www.thenews.com.pk/print/184916-Hate-speech-is-not-free-speech

Nina Burleigh. "The Battle Against 'Hate Speech' on College Campuses Gives Rise to a Generation That Hates Speech." *Newsweek*, May 26, 2016. http://www.newsweek.com/2016/06/03/college-campus-free-speech-thought-police-463536.html

Lauren Carroll. "CNN's Chris Cuomo: First Amendment doesn't cover hate speech." Politifact, May 7, 2015. http://www.politifact.com/punditfact/statements/2015/may/07/chris-cuomo/cnns-chris-cuomo-first-amendment-doesnt-cover-hate/

Lily Harmon. "What You Need to Know About Hate Speech and Free Speech." *Teen Vogue*, February 3, 2017. http://www.teenvogue.com/story/what-you-need-to-know-about-hate-speech-and-free-speech

Amanda Hoover. "Free speech vs. hate speech: How Reddit navigates the crosscurrents." *Christian Science Monitor*, December 1, 2016. http://www.csmonitor.com/USA/Society/2016/1201/Free-speech-vs.-hate-speech-How-Reddit-navigates-the-crosscurrents

Solveig Horne. "Hate Speech – A Threat to Freedom of Speech." *Huffington Post*, March 8, 2016. http://www.huffingtonpost.com/solveig-horne/hate-speech--a-threat-to_b_9406596.html

Frederick M. Lawrence. "A guide for colleges navigating the 'hate speech' line." The Hill, January 30, 2017. http://thehill.com/blogs/pundits-blog/education/316904-a-guide-for-colleges-navigating-the-hate-speech-line

Andrew Liptak. "Leslie Jones: 'hate speech and freedom of speech are two different things.'" The Verge, July 22, 2016. http://www.theverge.com/2016/7/22/12260256/leslie-jones-twitter-hate-speech-abuse-seth-meyers

Michael McGough. "Sorry, kids, the 1st Amendment does protect 'hate speech.'" *Los Angeles Times*, October 30, 2015. http://www.latimes.com/opinion/opinion-la/la-ol-colleges-hate-speech-1st-amendment-20151030-story.html

Elizabeth J. Meyer Ph.D. "Free Speech vs. Hate Speech." Psychology Today, December 5, 2016. https://www.psychologytoday.com/blog/gender-and-schooling/201612/free-speech-vs-hate-speech

Public Affairs. UC Berkeley. "Free Speech? Hate Speech? Or both?" *Berkeley News*, January 31, 2017. http://news.berkeley.edu/2017/01/31/free-speech-hate-speech-yiannopoulos/

The Editorial Board. "Free Speech vs. Hate Speech." *New York Times*, May 6, 2015. https://www.nytimes.com/2015/05/07/opinion/free-speech-vs-hate-speech.html

Eric Tucker. "How federal law draws a line between free speech and hate crimes." PBS, December 31, 2015. http://www.pbs.org/newshour/rundown/how-federal-law-draws-a-line-between-free-speech-and-hate-crimes/

Index

Solon Public Library
320 W. Main
Solon, IA 52333